The Complete Job Search Book

THE COMPLETE JOB SEARCH BOOK

RICHARD H. BEATTY

WILEY

John Wiley & Sons

New York   Chichester   Brisbane   Toronto   Singapore

This publication is designed to provide accurate and
authoritative information in regard to the subject
matter covered. It is sold with the understanding that
the publisher is not engaged in rendering legal, accounting,
or other professional service. If legal advice or other
expert assistance is required, the services of a competent
professional person should be sought. *From a Declaration
of Principles jointly adopted by a Committee of the
American Bar Association and a Committee of Publishers.*

Library of Congress Cataloging in Publication Data:

Beatty, Richard H., 1939–
 The complete job search book.

 Bibliography: p.
 1. Job hunting. I. Title.
HF5382.7.B42 1988   650.1'4   87-34512

ISBN 0-471-62869-7
ISBN 0-471-60250-7 (pbk.)

Printed in the United States of America

10 9 8 7 6 5 4 3

To my family

whose support and patience
were greatly appreciated this
summer, as I labored with
the writing of this book

Preface

This book has been written for those who are about to enter the job market and are in need of practical advice and guidance on how to organize and carry out an effective job hunting campaign. Whether you are a novice job hunter or a seasoned veteran, the concepts and ideas contained in this book should prove particularly helpful in planning and implementing a thorough, comprehensive, and hard-hitting job search campaign that will serve you well in today's highly competitive job market.

The emphasis of this book is on "practical application" rather than "theory." It has been organized in a logical, step-by-step fashion covering each step of the job hunting process in the order in which it should be carried out to ensure maximum effectiveness. Key topics include: formulating the job objective, picking the right résumé, preparing to write the résumé, résumé writing (several samples provided), utilizing employment sources (14 sources discussed), conducting a direct mail campaign, utilizing the networking process (the most effective job hunting source), strategies for effective interviewing, negotiating the job offer, and selecting the right employer.

Whether the subject is résumé writing, interviewing, or employment networking, I think the reader will appreciate the practical, "how to" approach taken in this book. In each case I have taken great care to outline a logical, step-by-step approach to be followed by the reader. By following these steps in the order presented, the reader is practically guaranteed a highly effective end product and a very positive result.

The advice and counsel in job hunting techniques presented in this book are the result of the author's more than 20 years of practical, first-hand experience as both a human resources and employment professional. This includes over four years experience in the field of executive search consulting, where I have helped several U.S. and foreign-based companies recruit, evaluate, and hire a wide range of managerial and executive talent. Previous experience includes over 17 years in Human Resources with Scott Paper Company, a Fortune 100 consumer products company, where I held several managerial positions, including Corporate Manager of Technical Employment and Manager of Human Resources for the Corporate Staff.

In the last 20 years, I estimate that I have read over 50,000 employment résumés, conducted well over 1500 employment interviews and participated in the recruitment, evaluation, and hiring of several hundred persons ranging from hourly worker, to technical professional, to manager, to director, to vice president, to president and chief executive officer. Likewise, my employment experience has covered a wide range of functional areas including art, fund raising, accounting, finance, marketing, sales, manufacturing, engineering, research & development, material management, management information services, human resources, and so on.

Over the years, I have had the opportunity to make numerous first hand observations about the various elements of the job hunting process—to observe what works and what doesn't. I have made these observations, not as a theorist from afar but as an experienced practitioner who has actively participated in the employment process both as a manager and as a consultant. I have attempted to share the benefit of this experience and the practical observations that I have made over the years concerning effective job hunting techniques with the reader.

I firmly believe that, if you carefully follow the step-by-step process outlined in this book, you will be successful in planning and implementing a very professional, effective, and hard-hitting job hunting campaign that will result in a highly successful outcome. Remember, however, there are no short cuts to an effective campaign. In job hunting there is no substitute for good organization, solid planning, thorough execution, dedication, and plain hard work. Armed with these characteristics and the advice and suggestions contained in this book, the odds are substantially in your favor that you will come out a winner.

Best wishes for a very successful job search and a professionally rewarding, satisfying career!

RICHARD H. BEATTY

West Chester, Pennsylvania
January 1988

Contents

Contents

1

Introduction

There is a certain logic to the steps of the job hunting process. Each step is a prelude to the next. In many ways, it resembles the construction of a building. You start with the excavation, then the foundation, then the first course of blocks, and so on, until the building is complete. Each step is a prerequisite to the next, and all are critical to the whole undertaking. Should any of these steps be omitted or performed out of sequence, the structure can be weakened and the project placed in jeopardy.

Much the same can be said of job hunting. There are certain steps that should be followed, and a set sequence that is vital to the success of the job search process. Disregard for these steps, or deviation from their proper sequence, can substantially undermine the entire procedure.

This book provides a step-by-step system for finding a job. Each step is presented in appropriate order, and, if followed, should automatically result in the creation and execution of a highly effective job search campaign. This step-by-step, building block approach is much like the directions in a kit and thus accounts for the title of the book.

The first step of the job hunting process is the establishment of the job objective. Without a distinct job objective, the job hunting strategy will lack direction and focus, and is bound to fail. Chapter 2 provides some helpful advice on how to formulate a well-defined job objective, which will serve as the nucleus of your job hunting campaign.

Having defined your job objective, you can then design a replete and effective résumé. The subject of résumé preparation, a principal component of any job search campaign, is covered in depth in Chapters 2 through 7. In order to increase appreciation for the difference between a good résumé and a bad résumé, Chapter 3 provides samples of both. This is then followed by instructions on résumé selection, advance preparation, and actual résumé composition. Several résumé samples are available for your review and reference.

A well-written résumé is clearly essential to launching your job quest. With this document in hand, you are prepared to contact employment sources and begin your actual campaign. A prime aspect of the search process at this point is knowing what employment sources to contact, and how to efficiently use them. Chapter 8, Employment Sources—How to Use Them, is packed full of valuable information. This chapter provides detailed descriptions of fourteen key employment source categories that should form a vital part of your job search. It also provides suggestions on how to maximize use of these important sources.

Two methods employed in most successful job searches are the direct mail campaign and the networking process. Because of their importance, Chapters 9 and 10 have been devoted exclusively to them. The *how to* approach used therein should make it fairly easy for you to learn and apply both techniques.

With these employment sources and methods in full swing, it will just be a matter of time before you'll surface some leads and the opportunity for that all-important job interview. Don't leave the interview to chance. Make sure that you are well-prepared. Chapter 11, Effective Interviewing, deals not only with how to prepare for the employment interview, but also provides specific interview strategies which, if well executed, can provide you with significant competitive advantage.

Successful interviews, of course, lead to job offers and negotiations. What are the guidelines for favorable negotiations? How does one prepare? What are some of the most effective techniques? These and related topics are the subject of Chapter 12, Negotiating.

Once negotiations have been completed and you have an acceptable offer in hand, how do you know if this is truly the right opportunity for you? Chapter 13 provides some practical methods to evaluate both the job and the employer to determine if this will be a *good fit*. It discusses several issues that need to be considered in addressing this matter, and provides some specific approaches that should prove helpful in reaching a satisfactory resolution.

As you can see, each of the chapter topics presented in this book is an integral part of the overall job search process. You will need to become intimately familiar with each if you are to conduct a well-planned and effective job hunting campaign.

2

Defining Your Job Objective

The job search process works best when it is structured around well-defined career goals. Job hunting is no easy process, and until goals are distinctly clarified, the process stands little chance of success. Job searchers with vague objectives will spend much of their time drifting aimlessly like rudderless ships in the ocean. They will be at the mercy of the winds and tides, with little or no control over their ultimate destination. There is no telling on what strange land they may run aground.

In the job search process, little can be gained from lack of focus. When a job is found under such circumstances, it is very likely that it will be lacking the challenge and satisfaction that most people require for long term job stability.

This chapter is about avoiding the aforementioned scenario. It will provide some practical suggestions and advice about how to set job goals that are meaningful. The competitive nature of the marketplace demands that your job search be structured around well-defined objectives if you are to be successful in your bid for desirable employment. In fact, your job goal is the very centerpiece of your job search design and provides the focus necessary to successful planning.

For a job hunting campaign to work, there must be a plan. For this plan to work, there must be a goal. All job hunting resources must be properly focused to maximize the probability for success. The goal provides the basis for such focus and thus is critical to the job search plan.

CAREER TESTING SERVICES

If you are just starting your career and are in a quandry about what to do with your life, I strongly recommend use of a good career testing and counseling service. You will find this to be money well spent.

Because there are several private firms that provide this type of consulting service, it may be difficult to distinguish between the professionals and the charlatans. I would recommend that you look into the career testing and counseling services provided by reputable universities. Many of these offer services to not only the student body but the general public as well. Fees may vary substantially, but you should be able to get this kind of assistance for somewhere in the $150 to $500 range.

Most of these university programs offer a day or two of intense testing followed by individual counseling. Tests normally examine IQ, personality, aptitude, and interest. This program is usually housed in the university's psychology department, and counselors are advanced degreed psychologists with specific training in career counseling.

One customary result of these tests is a comparison of your personal traits, interests and aptitudes with those who are successfully employed in a wide range of occupations. By making these comparisons, the psychologist is able to suggest various occupations that appear to be particularly suited to your specific profile. Conversely, you are counseled to avoid certain occupations that do not appear suitable, based upon this profile comparison method.

In any event, these career testing and counseling programs are usually quite effectual in helping one narrow down the choices. Following such counseling, a little practical research, including visitations with persons now employed in the recommended occupations, can usually narrow the field considerably more and allow you to select a career objective.

ELEMENTS OF SUCCESSFUL GOAL SETTING

The elements of successful job goal setting are as follows:

1. Goals must be realistic.
2. Goals must be achievable.
3. Goals must be well-defined.

If any of these elements is missing, there is a good possibility that the entire job search process will flounder and eventually fail. Let's examine each of these elements in greater detail.

Realistic

It is important, when establishing your job goal, that this goal be realistic. It would be unrealistic for someone with only two years of experience, to think that he or she could land a job at the vice-presidential level. It would be equally outrageous to think that someone without a degree in chemistry could work as a research chemist in a major company. These are unreasonable goals and, as such, are likely not achievable.

If you are interested in a certain career area and are uncertain whether you are being realistic in your expectations, I would suggest that you seek the practical advice of someone who is already employed in such a position. Or, you might consider discussing the matter with a seasoned employment professional who has hired numerous people into your targeted position.

With appropriate advice from knowledgeable sources, you may find that you need to readjust your sights to a lower and more fitting position.

Achievable

There are many who would like to be President of the United States. Simply wanting to be President doesn't mean that this is an achievable objective. Desire alone is not enough to accomplish your goals; you must also have the necessary skills and experience to make achievement possible. If your job objective is to be attainable, your qualifications must be sufficient enough to warrant serious consideration. Without these prerequisites, your job search will most certainly end in frustration.

Here again, it is important for you to seek some knowledgeable advice, should you have questions concerning the accessibility of your desired career. It is best to seek such advice from persons already employed in such capacity or from those who frequently are involved in hiring persons for such positions.

Well–defined

It is not enough for a job objective to be realistic and achievable; it must also be well-defined. It is difficult to build a meaningful job search strategy if your job objective is too obscure. For the most desirable results, your job objective should be specific in the following dimensions:

1. Organizational level
2. Functional area
3. Specialty (if required)
4. Industry
5. Geography

Using these parameters, a proper statement of objective would be:

> I seek a position as Director of Corporate Accounting in the banking or financial management field located in the northeastern United States.

This is a well-defined objective that will allow you to maximize the job search planning process and focus your job search resources for optimal results.

In contrast, consider this poorly defined objective:

> I seek a director level position in the financial field.

As you can readily see, it will be much more difficult to put together a meaningful job search strategy to meet this objective than in the preceding example. Without definition of the functional specialty and geographical zone, the job objective is so vague that a meaningful job search plan becomes very difficult to draft.

It should also be pointed out that the lack of a well-defined objective will also impair the preparation of a good résumé. A résumé based on an indistinct objective can not be properly tailored to showcase your relevant skills, capabilities and experience. Likewise, it will make it harder to plan a decent interview strategy. Overall, a poorly defined job objective will substantially reduce the effectiveness of your entire job search campaign.

ESTABLISHING YOUR OWN OBJECTIVE

Using the advice and guidelines provided in this chapter, try writing your own statement of job hunting objective by completing the following statement:

I seek a position as _____ in the _____
field located in _____.

Now test whether this objective is realistic and achievable by asking yourself the following questions:

1. Does my current job level support the job level that I am seeking?

2. Does my level of experience support the job level that I am seeking?

3. Do my qualifications (education, knowledge, skills, experience) support the functional area and specialty that I am seeking?

4. Will I be able to successfully compete with other qualified persons competing for this position?

5. Is my job objective both realistic and achievable?

If you have been able to answer each of these questions in the affirmative, you have formed a realistic, achievable, and well-defined job objective around which to structure a job search campaign. Having established this job objective, your next step in the job search process is employment résumé preparation. The next few chapters will deal with the subject of résumé selection and preparation, a very important part of the job hunting process.

3

Bad Résumés / Good Résumés

Writing an effective résumé is no accident. It doesn't just happen. One cannot expect to sit down the night before that all-important interview and write a résumé that will amply represent his or her background, including education, knowledge, skills, and relevant experience. Such crash attempts usually fall miserably short of the mark and, instead of creating a favorable impression, serve to scuttle the interview even before it gets started.

Résumé writing requires careful thought and planning. As a vital part of your job search, it is a task that deserves your maximum effort.

RÉSUMÉ PURPOSE

What is the role of the résumé in the employment process? How is it used and by whom?

Knowing the answer to these, and similar questions, is paramount to a well-formulated résumé. It is important to design a résumé that will meet the needs of the interviewer/employer—one that is easily read and focuses on those items cogent to the employer's evaluation and selection process.

Before proceeding with the résumé preparation process, it is important to have a thorough understanding of what this document is intended to accomplish. Unfortunately, many employment candidates have a somewhat narrow understanding of the role of the résumé, and therefore, end up with something that is inappropriate, at best.

The primary purpose of the résumé is to serve as a tool in helping you secure an employment interview. It must therefore convince a prospective employer that you are an outstanding candidate, who has something of value to contribute to the organization, and that it will be well worth his or her time to grant you a personal interview. The key word here is *value*. The résumé must convey that somehow the company's performance and profitability will be enhanced by hiring you.

Therefore, the résumé should emphasize your major contributions and accomplishments. It must not simply state the names of past employers and list the job titles of past positions that you have held. These factors alone cannot be expected to convince an employer of your merit. Instead, your résumé must convince the employer that you are someone who will bring improvements and make worthwhile contributions through the solution of major problems and issues confronting the organization. Only past accomplishments will serve to *make the sale*.

Although the primary function of the résumé is to help you to secure an employment interview, it also serves two important additional purposes as well:

1. First, it serves as a road map for your employment interview. In most cases, the interviewer will use it as an outline to guide the discussion, and to focus on those aspects of your qualifications that you have chosen to highlight.

2. Second, after the interview has taken place and you have departed, the interviewer will use the résumé as a reference source for recalling and/or further evaluating your specific strengths and abilities, as well as comparing them to others who are being considered for the position.

Keeping in mind these functions, it is easy to understand just how critical the résumé is to the outcome of the employment process. It should also be evident to you that, while preparing this important document, you will need to pay particular attention to its sales appeal. If it is to convince a prospective employer to interview and hire you, it must present your qualifications in the most favorable light, focusing on past accomplishments and results. Additionally, it must continue to remind the prospective employer of your excellent qualifications and value long after the interview discussion has been concluded.

CHARACTERISTICS OF POOR RÉSUMÉS

What are the differences between a good résumé and a bad résumé? By being aware of these distinctions, you will be better prepared to critique your own résumé and avoid the common pitfalls of bad résumé preparation.

What are the characteristics of poor résumés? Here are some that commonly account for résumé ineffectiveness:

1. Poor Organization—difficult to read (see Résumé A)

2. Sloppiness—conveys carelessness (see Résumé B)

3. Narrative Approach—too much time to read (see Résumé C)

4. Job Function vs Accomplishments Focus—fails to sell capability (see Résumé D)

5. Insufficient Information—can't fully evaluate (see Résumé E)

6. Too Much Information—too much time to read (see Résumé F)

7. Puffery and Bragging—insults employer's intelligence (see Résumé G)

Let's now examine these characteristics more closely so that you can clearly see their disadvantages.

Poor Organization

Résumé A on the next page is an example of poor organization. Visual examination alone shows the following disadvantages:

1. Is difficult to read

2. Takes too much time to read

3. Key information difficult to locate

4. Suggests writer is disorganized and does not think clearly

Obviously, this kind of résumé does little to improve your chances of landing a job interview, let alone providing the foundation for a successful one. You can be sure, with such a poor résumé, that the employer will be compelled to use much of your valuable interview time simply trying to ferret out basic information about your background. Little interview time will likely be left to explore your unique skills and value. A poorly organized résumé therefore, puts you at a distinct disadvantage as it devitalizes your interview.

As you can see, a little organization can go a long way to improving your employment chances. Take time to develop a well-organized résumé.

Investment Banker with 17 year record of success in Mergers, Acquisitions, Joint Ventures and Capital Formation now seeking to apply skills in corporate situation. International experience, multi-lingual, U.S. citizen. Young, articulate, presents self well. Pleasant, friendly, people-oriented.

David K. Larson
H: 512/337-9872
W: 512/887-9823

325 Pierson Street
Detroit, MI 22398

Current Responsibilities

Relocating to Atlanta in 1983, I established an independent consulting practice making use of my skills in:

-Business Development
-Transaction analysis
-Industry search

-Valuations
-Negotiations
-Debt and equity financing

My successes here (since 1983) include:
   *Major transactions and new development of hotels in Atlanta, Tampa, Mobile, New Orleans and Miami.
   *Expansion of sewer service through industrial revenue development bonds.
   *Refinancing development of waste disposal facilities through I.D.R. bonds.

Earlier Accomplishments

As Vice President Zebco Enterprises on the West Coast (1978-1983):
   -Successfully invested $2.5 million in several real estate development transactions, some with debt to equity ratio of 25 to 1.
      *Sell-outs averaged up to 200% return for investors.
As Vice President of Consolidated Enterprises in Boston (1974-78):
   -Successfully accomplished leveraged buy-out of a candy manufacturer, flour blending plant, four hotels, two land parcels, manufacturer of frozen pastries as well as several homes
      *All purchases proved profitable
      (up to 200% return) for investors.
From 1970-74, I managed investments in Kenya for an investor group seeking Black nationals to buy businesses owned by whites seeking to leave Africa.
   -Secured 100% financing for buyer's group for three major companies
      *Providing sellers cash purchase at full asking price.
Assigned management responsibilities for conglomerate (tour operators, hardware store, auto imports,finance company and service stations)
Added four new companies. Increased unit sales 12% and tripled corporate profitability.

Personal Background

Studying under the Cambridge University program while living in England, I completed a degree in Mathematics and, in 1970, finished first out of 18,000 taking tests for accreditation by the Association of Certified and Corporate Accountants. (C.P.A. equivalency) Only 18% passed the examination.

Continuing education includes ongoing program of related conferences and workshops. Regularly read a wide range of business and news publications.

Age 39, divorced, no dependents. Free to travel extensively.

Detailed references furnished upon request.

Résumé A—Poor Organization

Sloppiness

Résumé B is an example of sloppiness. In addition to a smudge mark and a coffee stain on the paper itself, the résumé is also poorly prepared. There are several spelling errors, missing words, irregular margins, inconsistent underlining of key sections, manual corrections, manual underlining, etc. Most employers, receiving a résumé in this condition, would simply not even bother to read it.

Among the many disadvantages of a sloppy résumé are:

1. Creates poor impression with employer
2. Is difficult to read
3. Detracts from content
4. Suggests writer is careless, irresponsible, and lacks personal pride
5. Suggests writer is prone to error, is inaccurate, and lacks thoroughness
6. Suggests writer lacks initiative and motivation

There is really no excuse for a sloppy résumé. If you are poor at spelling or grammar, seek the assistance of someone who is strong in these areas. Have your résumé proofread and make necessary corrections before it goes to press. Likewise, if you are a poor typist, take your résumé to a professional typist and have it done right.

Your résumé is usually the very first contact that an employer has with you. It is important, therefore, that it represents you as someone who is neat, thorough, accurate, organized, responsible, and well-motivated. A sloppy résumé creates the opposite impression and serves as a very real barrier to a successful employment campaign.

Richard R. Johnson
325 East Exton Stree
Richboro, Pennsylvannia 8872'

Phone: (313) 675-2371

Objective: To find a responsable posiition in Operations Management with a major manufacturing company.

Education: B.S. Degree, Industrial Engineering
University of Virginia, 1978

Work Experience:

1980-1987 **Manufacturing Manager**, Rammar Corporation, Philadelphia, Pennsylvannia.:
I report to the Derector of Manufacturing and managea 150 employee department engaged in the manufacture of printed circuit boards for computer-controlled drill presses. In the last 3 years have incresed output by 35% and redused Manufacturing costs by 18%, at the same time reducing employee headcount by 5%. Operating budget is $35 Million with value of goods manufacturied in the $62 range.
Million

1978-1980 **Shift Supervisor**, Duncan Corporation, Lansdale, PA. Worked two yeras as the Shift Supervisor for the ———> Rotor Division. Managed group of 27 hourly workers in the manufacture of stainless steel rotors for adverse environment motors.

Hobbies: Reading, running, sailing, fishing and card playing.

Professional Affiliations:
Member - Philadelphia Area Engineers' Club-1979 to present.
Member - Industrial Engineering Assoc. - 1980 to 1986

Personal:

Age   : 30
Height   : 5'10"
Weight   : 175 pounds
Marital Status: Single (Engaged)

Résumé B—Sloppiness

17

Narrative Approach

Résumé C is an example of the narrative approach. As you can see, this style reads very much like a letter and sets forth the candidate's background in paragraph form.

Although at first glance, this résumé may seem quite acceptable to the inexperienced job seeker, I can assure you that seasoned employment professionals do not share this feeling. For the person who must read your résumé and decide whether you warrant further consideration, there are several drawbacks to this type of résumé. They are as follows:

1. Takes too much time to read

2. Forces employer to read entire résumé in order to get key information (many won't bother)

3. Suggests writer does not have sufficient motivation or patience to write proper résumé

4. Suggests writer may be naive about proper résumé format and acceptable business protocol

5. Suggests writer may also be ignorant about other acceptable business practices and courtesies

6. Suggests the writer simply doesn't care

It should be evident that the job seeker places himself/herself at a real disadvantage when utilizing the narrative form of résumé. Using a proper résumé format will, in most cases, contribute to the success of your job search. So, take the time to research and utilize an acceptable résumé format, rather than simply using the narrative approach. This could spell the difference between a fruitful campaign and one that ends in failure.

1324 Donovan Terrace
Rockville, MD 97218

Phone: Office - (312) 893-1724
Home   - (312) 892-1754

I am a chemical engineer with an M.B.A. and have 20 years of experience to bring to a future employer.

Joining my current employer, Ace Chemical Corporation, a Fortune 100 firm, in 1967, I held operations management positions of increasing responsibility for ten years, including one year of insurance and development. In my most recent operations and engineering management positions, I supervised hourly and salaried personnel in production, maintenance, and shipping. I was also responsible for overseeing the environmental and water treatment functions for pH control in the production of caustic soda.

Earlier, I served as General Foreman in polymer production, where I supervised production operations, maintenance, shipping, and quality control including inventory of finished product, production equipment, and sales requirements. Prior to this, as Senior Operations Engineer, I was responsible for diverse technical projects for the improvement of production rates and quality, increased yields, reduction of operations and maintenance expenses, manpower reduction requirements, and supervision and training of equipment operators.

Previously, as Process Engineer, I served as liaison between production and R & D to resolve critical problems in the nylon product lines. This included preparing various economic studies on alternatives, plus bench scale and pilot scale studies, and full scale plant experiments of special operating parameters. As Operations Engineer, I supervised a staff of 85 equipment operators in the raw materials and unloading section, and performed analytical testing and studies in quality control and operating rates.

My recent experience, since 1979, in Product Management and Regional Sales and Marketing has encompassed significant responsibility. As Regional Manager, I achieved personal annual sales of $92 million to major accounts and, as Area Sales Manager, I was responsible for territories with annual sales up to $139 million. I developed sales and marketing strategies for several chemical products and managed a sales and clerical support staff in a 22 state region.

Personally, I am 45 years of age, married, have six children; and earned my M.B.A. degree from the University of Maryland, and my Chemical Engineering degree from Drexel University in Philadelphia. My present salary is $85,000 per year.

Résumé C—Narrative Approach

Job Function vs Accomplishments Focus

Résumé D focuses on job function rather than on the individual's accomplishments. Reading this is like reading a job description rather than a résumé. As you read it, you get the feeling that the résumé is more an account of the positions performed than it is a portrayal of the person who has performed them. Such a résumé is boring. Other adjectives which also come to mind are bland and inanimate. It does little to create any enthusiasm or excitement about the candidate and his/her capabilities.

Major disadvantages of this kind of résumé are:

1. Fails to sell candidate's capability
2. Focuses on functions performed rather than results achieved
3. Makes boring reading

Admittedly, this is not an altogether bad approach to résumé writing. It does at least list each position held along with an explanation of the functional responsibilities for which the candidate has been accountable. This does provide some basis for proper evaluation of the candidate.

The point is, however, that the résumé can be improved by adding some of the major accomplishments realized while the candidate was in these positions. The inference that is drawn by employers from such inclusion is that the candidate is well-motivated and results-oriented. This is in contrast with the person who is satisfied with the status quo and who will simply perform the job as it has always been performed. Instead, most companies would much prefer to hire persons who will make changes, bring improvement, and add value to the organization. Statements of results achieved, along with a description of functional responsibilities, clearly play an important role in developing a résumé that will be effective.

CATHERINE F. GILES
816 Wacker Avenue
Detroit, MI 19875

Phone: (422) 897-1141

Education:

Ph.D., Industrial Psychology
University of Michigan, 1968

M.S., Industrial Relations
Michigan State University, 1966

B.A., Human Resource Management
Michigan State University, 1964
Summa Cum Laude

Professional Experience:

1970 to Present   Paxton Motor Corporation, Corporate Offices
East Lansing, Michigan

1986 to Present   Vice President - Human Resources:
Report directly to the President of this 2,500
employee, $500 million manufacturer of specialty
motors. Manage staff of 35 with functional
responsibility for human resource planning,
organization design and development, training,
compensation and benefits, and E.E.O.

1980-1986   Director Human Resources - Recco Division:
Reported to Vice President Human Resources -
Corporate Staff. Responsibilities included wage and
salary administration, organization design, benefits
administration, labor relations, training and
development, safety and hygiene, and medical.

1975-1980   Personnel Manager - Kingston Plant:
Reported to Plant Manager with indirect
responsibility to the Director of Human Resources -
Recco Division. Was accountable for all plant H.R.
functions, including: wage and salary administration
employee relations, labor negotiations, training and
development, benefits, safety, hygiene and medical.

1970-1975   Consultant - Corporate Organization Effectiveness:
Reported to the Director of Organization
Development. Provided consulting support to both the
Recco and Stevens Divisions in the areas of
socio-technical system implementation, team
building and participatory management techniques.

Résumé D —Job Function vs Accomplishments Focus

1968–1970   <u>The Polaris Corporation, Overstad Division</u>
<u>East Lansing, Michigan</u>

Consultant - Organization Design:
Reported to the Corporate Director of Human
Resources. Provided consulting support in the area
of organization design and development.

Personal:

Age	:	47
Height	:	5'4"
Weight	:	140 pounds
Marital Status	:	Divorced, 3 Children
Health	:	Excellent

Résumé D —(Continued)

22

Insufficient Information

Résumé E is an example of insufficient information. Important data which most employers need for determining whether they have an interest in the candidate is missing. Use of such a résumé places the job hunter at a disadvantage when compared to other well-qualified candidates who have been more disclosing.

Key information that is missing from this résumé is as follows:

1. No statement of job objective

2. No statement of educational qualifications

3. No description of functional responsibilities for past positions held

4. No description of size and scope of positions held

5. No description of major results and accomplishments for each position previously held

As an experienced employment professional, who has worked for two executive search firms and a Fortune 200 company, I can tell you that the missing information cited here is what most seasoned employment professionals look for in a well constructed résumé. It is key information that is important to making a preliminary determination of interest in the candidate.

It is important that both the right amount and right kind of information be presented in the résumé if it is to serve you well in the interview process. Be careful, therefore, that your résumé is not incomplete.

Too Much Information

Having too much information in your résumé is as bad as, if not worse than, presenting the employer with insufficient information.

Ann C. Johnson
824 Spruce Street
Denver, Colorado 87723

Phone: (315) 267-8759 (O)
       (315) 267-8970 (H)

My MBA and early background in finance (CPA with strong commercial lending experience for a regional bank) enabled me to make the transition into general management easily. As a general manager, I have placed strong emphasis on sales/marketing, diversification of products, refinancing, and acquisitions/joint ventures. In summary, I have been the prime mover in corporate expansion and growth.

CAREER HIGHLIGHTS

* Increased sales by 75% in an industry where sales declined by 25%.

* Realized savings of $20,000 annually through installation and operation of new equipment and the negotiation of labor, purchasing, and financing contracts.

* Created unique loan packages and banking services, resulting in substantial return.

WORK HISTORY

Denver Bag Company
    1981 to Present - Exec. V.P. & Gen. Manager
    1979 to 1981   - Controller/Treasurer

First National Bank of Georgia
    1978 to 1979   - Assist. V.P. Commercial Loans

First National Bank of Denver
    1976 to 1978   - Section Head/Credit Analysis

Résumé E—Insufficient Information

Résumé F is an example of too much information. This approach places the job seeker at a very real disadvantage and should be avoided at all cost.

Notable problems with résumés of this sort are as follows:

1. Takes too much time to read

2. Key information not readily visible

3. Suggests writer lacks good judgment; lacks ability to separate the important from the unimportant

4. Suggests writer is unnecessarily verbose

5. Suggests writer may be naive about proper résumé format and acceptable business protocol

6. Suggests writer may also be ignorant of other acceptable business practices and courtesies or, worse yet, doesn't care

Each of the above is an excellent reason why the job hunter should avoid writing a résumé that is too long. Presenting a proper balance of information (i.e., not too much and not too little) is very essential to résumé effectiveness. Résumés that are either too long or too short can present a serious handicap to an otherwise productive job hunting campaign.

Puffery and Bragging

A candidate's use of puffery or bragging can substantially detract from an otherwise acceptable résumé. Résumé G is an example of such.

Although it has often been said that the employment interview is the time to brag, to toot your own horn (and I generally agree), this is not true of the employment résumé. The résumé is intended to

Allen B. Barber
226 Master Blvd.
Reading, PA 19886

Phone: (215) 875-9961

BSME, University of Pennsylvania, 1960
Pennsylvania Registration #55798
Member, National Society of Professional Engineers (NSPE)
Member, Society of Petroleum Engineers (SPE)
Member, American Society of Mechanical Engineers (ASME)

Personal: Currently employed with Scantia Technology.
References will be furnished upon request. Credible work
history maintained throughout career. Work generally
obtained through personal acquaintances. Work never left
unfinished or incomplete (except for companies discontinuing
operations.

Objective: Work career and senior level of
technical/administrative ability have endowed a combination
of highly diversifies skills and ready association with a
broad perspective of most problems encountered, i.e. all
prior assignments have varied considerably in scope. This
has produced the ability to perform immediately with little
(if any) learning curve. My objective is to obtain
challenging employment in a growth market and to apply my
above described credentials in continuation of a successful
career. This objective represents an interest in either
direct employment or as a consultant, and further includes
an open mind to domestic or international relocation.

EXPERIENCE OVERVIEW:

Excellent overall technical and administrative skills
founded upon twenty-seven years of involvement in numerous,
diversified market environments including: mechanical
designs, pneumatics/hydraulics, systems, testing,
developmental, reliability/quality control, construction,
analytical, manufacturing, management/administrative and
marketing.Most recent specialty areas include equipment
designs and systems engineering. Have been employed as an
independent consultant for past six years.

Résumé F—Too Much Information

<u>Market environments</u> reflecting the above acquired skills
include energy, aerospace, defense, utilities, and
manufactured housing.

<u>Titles include</u>: Consultant, Manager of Engineering (3
positions), Project Manager, Project Engineer, Design/Senior
Design Engineer, Reliability/Quality Control Engineer, Test
Engineer/Supervisor, Market Research Analyst, Senior Staff
Engineer, Manufacturing Engineer, Engineering Coordinator,
Systems Engineer, Stress Analyst, Piping Designer and
Draftsman.

<u>Employer Affiliations</u> include a wide range of blue chip
companies, many of which reflect contract work and
assignments in volatile, unstable job markets, i.e.
aerospace, defense and energy. Firms for which I have worked
include the following:

1987	Scantia Corporation	1972	Franklin Space Company
1986	Austin Latril	1971	Offshore Drilling Co.
1985	Houston Oil	1970	Tankland Corporation
1985	Tarracott Corp.	1969	California Energy Corp.
1984	Marshall Engineering	1968	Poe & Daggert Utilities
1983	Foster Wheeler Corp.	1967	Potter Engine Company
1982	Orvield Bach Co.	1966	General Electric Co.
1980	Carter Jet Engine Co.	1962	National Lead Company
1976	Ford Bacon Engineers	1960	Carson Instruments
1974	Eastman Kodak	1959	Litton Industries

EXPERIENCE DETAILS

<u>Mechanical Designs</u>: Prepared engineering, conceptual
designs, layouts, details and bills of materials for
numerous products including structural operating machinery,
material handling and piping systems for hydroelectric and
steam plants at TVA and Corps of Engineers. Also responsible
for flight hardware test equipment for Saturn engines,
instrument packages, launch support facilities, designs for
pneumatic/hydraulic panels and equipment installations at
NASA, Huntsville and the Cape. Involved in the design of
flight systems payload experimental hardware and Astronaut
crew systems equipment such as waste management, life
support systems, extra vehicular space suit, safety
equipment, utilities, bio-medical equipment and personal
garments for duration of Apollo, Skylab, and briefly for the

Résumé F—(Continued)

3

Shuttle programs. Heavy background in rotating equipment
such as pumps, gas compressors, turbines, co-generation
packages, valves, piping systems, skid-mounted packages,
including all structural, instrumentation, piping equipment
and materials selections. Provided process design of all oil
and gas production equipment, engineered mechanical
equipment for offshore drilling and production subsea, and on
platforms; designed new development hardware such as
acoustic inspection device, subsea hydraulic control
packages, Arctic drilling systems, subsea pumping, subsea
process and new methods involving improved
efficiencies/reliability. Designed commercial air
conditioning system while overseas (Saudi Arabia).

SYSTEMS: Systems engineering, analysis and evaluations
involving Astronaut crew systems interface with flight
hardware; NASA payload systems reliability interface
involving failure mode analysis for a variety of flight
equipment, space hardware configuration control interface,
NASA launch support systems facility interface; NASA/DOD
hardware system milestone reviews with vendors. Engineered
oil and gas package drilling and production systems for land
and subsea, including controls, process, safety, maintenance
and operations (there were numerous equipment subsystems,
all of which functioned as a total system). Also, reviewed
and checked drawings of complete assemblies/details.

TESTING: Supervised group responsible for environmental
simulation testing of Apollo flight hardware at the Langston
Flight Center, including failure analysis. Supervised
testing of Skylab flight hardware used by Astronauts at
Johnson Space Center. Engaged in testing of flight hardware
on classified DOD project at Eastman Kodak. Responsible for
systems testing (land and subsea) of hydraulic/pneumatic
control packages and power packages. Responsible for
rotating equipment and valve testing including failure,
pressure, functional and systems. Responsible for numerous
packaged systems customer acceptance tests.

RELIABILITY/QUALITY ASSURANCE: Responsible for vendor
compliance with NASA reliability and quality assurance codes
and standards for assigned flight hardware including medical
experiments and crew equipment while with Carter Company.
Prepared failure effects analysis (FMEA) and failure
analysis.

ANALYTICAL: Good analytical skills in a variety of fields
spanning refrigeration and air conditioning, structural

Résumé F—(Continued)

stress analysis, piping stress analysis, mechanical equipment designs and selections, power trains, pneumatics/hydraulics, computer applications and process designs.

MANUFACTURING: Numerous manufacturing environments including nuclear weapons production, valve and mechanical equipment manufacturing and manufacturing of packaged skid-mounted mechanical systems. Skills utilized included drawing compliance, quality assurance, reliability, machining operations, welding, tolerances, dimensional buildup, scheduling etc.

CONSTRUCTION: Served as construction site engineer with Carter steam plant in Pennsylvania, supervising mechanical equipments installations. Served as construction engineer for numerous oil and gas, mechanical and process packages from one to several hundred tons installed on platforms. Served as construction coordinator for waste water treatment plant in Philadelphia.

MARKETING: Heavy marketing skills throughout career. Wide variety of proposal management activities too numerous to describe, including technical writing and editing, heavy budgeting and estimating experience, and scheduling associated with proposals. Diverse markets such as search lights for helicopters, solar cells and solar astronomical instruments are included.

ADMINISTRATIVE: Manager of engineering departments for two major mechanical equipment manufacturers (approximately 60 people in each department) and a consultant company. Contracts administrator for aerospace equipment with NASA contractors; served on contract negotiating teams. Served in numerous project management positions with cost responsibility for engineering of up to $2 million, including purchasing, scheduling, clerical etc.

CODE FAMILIARITY: ASME, ANSI, MMS, API, NFPA, ASHRAE, AISC, ASTM. Experience also with MIL-STD, DOD and NASA standards.

Résumé F—(Continued)

present a factual chronology of your background; it is not intended as a medium for extolling your many virtues. It is simply intended to present an honest account of where you've been and what you've accomplished.

To the experienced employment professional, attempts at self-evaluation in the résumé document are usually seen as amateurish at best and, at worst, downright insulting. Seasoned professionals prefer to make their own evaluation of a candidate's strengths and weaknesses, and are sometimes resentful of an attempt to influence their judgment in what they consider to be a proprietary area which is their sole domain. Use of puffery and bragging in the résumé compounds and intensifies these feelings.

Key disadvantages of using bragging or puffery in the résumé are as follows:

1. Suggests writer is insensitive to professional role of interviewer

2. Suggests writer is unaware of proper business practice and acceptable protocol

3. Suggests writer considers interviewer naive

4. Wastes valuable space that could be better used to further describe functional responsibilities, job scope, and major accomplishments

Although puffery or bragging should never be used, should you wish to delineate your major strengths, the cover letter that accompanies your résumé is a far more appropriate place to accomplish this objective. Under no circumstances, however, use the résumé to accomplish this.

Linda B. Carver
421 South Warren Street
Chicago, IL 87326

Phone: (315) 473-9872

OBJECTIVE: Controller for major hospital or other health care institution.

MAJOR STRENGTHS:

* Adjust well to rapidly changing environments and circumstances.

* Professional...Responsible...Accurate...Thorough.

* A creative problem solver...analytical, decisive.

* Highly creative, innovative, resourceful.

* Very responsive to pressure and deadlines.

* Known for getting superior results and delivering highest quality work.

* Personable, exceptionally well-liked...get along with everybody.

* High energy, forceful, dynamic, results-oriented.

EDUCATION:

M.S., Accounting & Finance
University of Wisconsin, 1969

B.A., Business Administration
Western Michigan University, 1967

EMPLOYMENT HISTORY:

1978-1987   Chicago Memorial Hospital, Chicago, IL

1982-1987   Hospital Administrator
1978-1982   Controller

Résumé G—Puffery and Bragging

1972-1978   <u>Saint Francis Hospital, Naperville, IL</u>

1974-1978   Assistant Controller

1972-1974   Senior Accountant

1969-1972   <u>Keefer Nursing Home, Chicago, IL</u>

Accountant

<u>PERSONAL</u>:

```
Age              : 41
Height           : 6'2"
Weight           : 225 pounds
Marital Status: Married, 3 Children
Health           : Excellent
```

Résumé G—(Continued)

CHARACTERISTICS OF GOOD RÉSUMÉS

We have now had a fairly thorough review of bad résumés, and I have shared a number of examples with you. But what about good résumés? What makes an employment résumé effective?

It will probably come as little surprise that the characteristics of good résumés are the opposite of poor résumés. The good résumé is carefully written to incorporate certain characteristics that, in themselves, assure that the final product will be both professional and meaningful.

Key characteristics of good résumés are as follows:

1. Neat
2. Well-organized
3. Easily and quickly read
4. Key information highly visible
5. Proper length—not too long, not too short
6. Includes brief, but complete job descriptions
7. Depicts key accomplishments
8. Comprehensive—provides complete accounting of key areas of interest to prospective employers

Résumé H is an example of a good résumé. You will note that it is exceptionally neat and well-organized. This résumé is easily read, and key information is highly visible. Even though it spans close to 25 years, it can be read quickly and all relevant information is at the employer's fingertips.

When reviewing Résumé H, you will note that each position held by the candidate is fully described, including reporting relationship,

WARREN P. SLOAN
825 Summit Avenue
Wyomissing, PA 19872

Phone: (215) 775-0967

OBJECTIVE: Senior level position in Operations management in medium-sized manufacturing company.

EDUCATION:

M.S., Pennsylvania State University, 1965
Major: Mechanical Engineering

B.S., Pennsylvania State University, 1963
Major: Mechanical Engineering
Grade Point Average: 3.7/4.0
Tau Beta Psi

WORK HISTORY:

1975 to Present   **WELLINGTON TUBE CORPORATION (CORPORATE OFFICES)**

Vice President of Manufacturing (1980 to Present)
Report to President with full P&L responsibility for two copper refineries and tube manufacturing plants for this leading producer of copper tubing (annual sales $500 million). Direct the activities of two Plant Managers, 300 salaried and 5,000 hourly employees with annual budget of $300 million. Organized and directed cost reduction task force which identified and implemented programs resulting in 22% reduction in manufacturing costs in 3 years ($60 million savings). Implemented computerized materials scheduling and control system which cut raw materials inventories by 30% (annual savings $15 million).

WELLINGTON TUBE CORPORATION (NORFOLK PLANT)

Plant Manager (1975 to 1980)
Reported to Vice President of Manufacturing with full P&L responsibility for this 3,000 employee copper refinery and tube manufacturing plant ($375 million annual production). Functions reporting included manufacturing, materials management, distribution, maintenance, engineering, accounting and personnel. Successfully directed two year, $125 million expansion program which doubled plant's production capacity (all engineering done at plant level). Project completed on time and 10% under budget. Set plant production and safety records for four out of five years.

Résumé H—Good Résumé

1970 to 1975	DOBBLER COPPER COMPANY, INC. (CORPORATE OFFICES)

Manager of Engineering

Managed 150 employee Central Engineering function for this manufacturer of refrigeration tubing (annual sales $250 million). Directed engineering organization in all capital project expansion programs to include design, installation, start-up and debugging of copper tube manufacturing facilities and refineries. Successfully engineered major $125 million capital program (largest in company's history) including installation and start-up of state-of-the-art, computer controlled, integrated refinery and tube mill. Project delivered four months ahead of schedule and on budget.

1965 to 1970	ZACKRISON COPPER & BRASS COMPANY (WARREN PLANT)

Department Manager, Drawing Operation (1968-1970)

Managed 100 employee tube drawing operation with annual production valued at $85 million. Increased production by 15% with simultaneous 8% reduction in manufacturing costs in 2 year period.

Project Engineer (1965-1968)

Responsible for design, installation and start-up of major capital projects in furnace and drawing operations. Independently handled projects in the $10-15 million range.

PERSONAL:
Married, 1 Child
U.S. Citizen
Excellent Health

REFERENCES:
Excellent references furnished upon request.

Résumé H—(Continued)

scope and size of position, and key job responsibilities. Likewise, for each position held, there is some description of major accomplishments or results achieved by the candidate. There is thus a good balance between functional description and accomplishments, suggesting someone who is well-motivated and results-oriented.

Hopefully, this chapter has served to convince you of the importance of a good résumé to your overall job hunting campaign. The ensuing chapters will now walk you through each of the steps necessary to prepare an effective résumé. Focus will be on the two most popular formats—the reverse chronological résumé and the functional résumé.

4

Résumé Writing — Advance Preparation

For most people, the task of writing a résumé does not come easily. It is, at best, an unnatural process. There are few times in our lives when we are required to write about ourselves, and many find this an embarrassing process. By contrast, we are frequently called upon to write various business letters and reports. This is a process that most of us find considerably easier.

Taking a few moments to reflect on what is causing this anxiety will usually yield some fairly consistent answers as follows:

1. Lack knowledge of résumé content (what to say or not say)

2. Lack knowledge of proper format (how to organize the résumé)

3. Lack knowledge of proper style (how to express it)

If you know what to say, how to organize it, and how to express it, there should be little reason to feel uncomfortable about the résumé process. In addition, the more you have prepared and rehearsed, the more comfortable you will feel in your ability to write a suitable résumé. This chapter is designed to assist you in developing these preparation skills, and the confidence to move on to the actual writing.

Moreover, the direction of this chapter will be twofold. First, we will focus on systematically gathering the necessary data about you and your background. Second, we will focus on writing skills, i.e., how to word the résumé to achieve maximum effectiveness. The subject of format (how to organize the résumé) will be dealt with in the subsequent chapters entitled *The Reverse Chronological Résumé* and *The Functional Résumé*.

PERSONAL DATA

Before you can proceed with the actual process of résumé writing, you will need to have a considerable amount of personal data at your fingertips. Further, these facts must be organized in such a manner as to be easily accessible when you need them. This advance preparation is essential to assuring an orderly, efficient résumé process. It is intended to save you time and frustration.

The following forms have been designed to assist you in systematically collecting the key information that you will need to have available once the actual writing process begins.

Professional Experience

Directions   Starting with your most recent employer, list all previous employment: dates of employment, name of employer, division for which you worked, title of position held, title of person to

Education

Starting with your most recent degree, fill in each of the spaces provided.

Degree _____

School _____ Date graduated _____

Major _____ Grade point average _____

Minor _____ Grade point average _____

Honoraries _____
_____
_____

Scholarships _____
_____
_____

Publications _____
_____
_____

Offices held _____
_____
_____

Professional Credentials

Professional Certification

Professional certification license _____

Date certified or licensed _____

Certifying organization _____

Professional certification license _____

Date certified or licensed _____

Certifying organization _____

Professional Memberships

Name of organization _____

Membership dates   From _____ to _____

Offices held _____
_____

Name of organization _____

Membership dates   From _____ to _____

Offices held _____
_____

Name of organization _____

Membership dates   From _____ to _____

Offices held _____
_____

1. Dates Employed   From _____ to _____

   Employer   _____

   Division   _____

   Position title   _____

   Reported to   _____

   Responsibilities   _____

   _____

   _____

   _____

   Accomplishments _____

   _____

   _____

2. Dates Employed   From _____ to _____

   Employer   _____

   Division   _____

   Position title   _____

   Reported to   _____

   Responsibilities   _____

   _____

   _____

   _____

   Accomplishments _____

   _____

   _____

3. Dates Employed   From _____ to _____

   Employer _____

   Division _____

   Position title _____

   Reported to _____

   Responsibilities _____

   _____

   _____

   _____

   Accomplishments _____

   _____

   _____

4. Dates Employed   From _____ to _____

   Employer _____

   Division _____

   Position title _____

   Reported to _____

   Responsibilities _____

   _____

   _____

   _____

   Accomplishments _____

   _____

   _____

5. Dates Employed   From _____ to _____

Employer   _____

Division   _____

Position title   _____

Reported to   _____

Responsibilities   _____

Accomplishments   _____

6. Dates Employed   From _____ to _____

Employer   _____

Division   _____

Position title   _____

Reported to   _____

Responsibilities   _____

Accomplishments   _____

Military Service

Dates served   From _____ to _____

Branch of service _____

Unit   _____

Rank at discharge _____

Date of discharge _____

Type of discharge _____

Community Service

Date   From _____ to _____

Organization _____

Offices held _____

Dates held   From _____ to _____

Date   From _____ to _____

Organization _____

Offices held _____

Dates held   From _____ to _____

Date   From _____ to _____

Organization _____

Offices held _____

Dates held   From _____ to _____

Hobbies/Activities

List all hobbies and activities in which you are currently active:

_____

_____

_____

whom you reported, job description (functional responsibilities and size/scope of position), and major accomplishments.

In those cases where you held more than one position with the same employer, write the word *same* in the space provided for the employer's name. Also, in those cases where you have held more than six positions, continue with this exercise on a separate piece of paper.

Unless you are a student, don't list summer jobs or part-time employment. Students, however, should include all summer, co-op, intern and part-time positions.

You have now collected the basic information that you will need to have available for the preparation of your résumé. This same information should also prove helpful as you approach your employment interview (which is discussed later in this book).

POWER WRITING

We are now transitioning our discussion of résumé content (what goes into the résumé) to résumé writing (how it is expressed). Writing style is a foremost factor in the résumé preparation process for three reasons:

1. Clarity—Information needs to be conveyed in a clear, concise manner that fosters good understanding and favorable communication.

2. Conciseness—Several years of experience need to be effectively condensed into a one or two-page format.

3. Forcefulness—Your message needs to be strong. It should have maximum impact in a minimum amount of space.

The art of saying things in a clear, concise and forceful manner is what I call *power writing*. Power writing is a well-advised technique that can give you the edge when competing with the myriad of résumés an employer must read.

Let's examine some of the basic principles of power writing. Having considered these principles, we will then review some examples of power writing to further emphasize its importance.

Rules of Power Writing

The fundamental rules of power writing are as follows:

1. Job Title—Avoid repeating your job title when describing your responsibilities and accomplishments. This is unnecessary since your title has already been stated as part of the résumé heading.

2. Pronoun *I*—Avoid using the pronoun *I* in the text of your résumé. Since this is your résumé, the I is understood.

3. Action Verbs—Where possible, start sentences with an action verb followed by a noun or an adjective. This forces brevity and conciseness.

4. Incomplete Sentences—In résumé writing, it is not always necessary to write in complete sentences to communicate effectively. This is particularly true since, in résumé writing, the pronoun *I* is understood. The use of descriptive phrases and clauses is acceptable as long as they convey a complete thought and are clearly understood.

5. Condense/Consolidate—Where possible, condense related information into a single statement rather than making separate statements. Eliminate all nonessential information which adds little or no meaning to your employment qualifications.

6. Quantitative Descriptions—Where possible, use quantitative terms to describe your position and accomplishments. This

provides a sense of dimension or magnitude that is helpful in conveying fuller understanding and also makes the résumé far more interesting to read.

Action Words

The following is a list of commonly used action words in résumé writing, and should prove helpful as a reference to you during the writing process:

Managed	Conducted	Composed	Structured
Administered	Approved	Developed	Organized
Directed	Implemented	Founded	Planned
Supervised	Controlled	Created	Consolidated
Lead	Coordinated	Invented	Originated
Guided	Motivated	Conceived	Designed
Solved	Evaluated	Produced	Improved
Optimized	Revised	Designed	Streamlined
Scheduled	Modified	Built	Accelerated
Maximized	Analyzed	Generated	Expanded
Monitored	Researched	Engineered	Increased
Proved	Revamped	Provided	Saved
Maintained	Trained	Decreased	Instructed
Sold	Accomplished	Completed	Presented
Began	Provided	Eliminated	Negotiated
Purchased	Performed	Finished	Contracted
Launched	Expedited	Canceled	Taught
Established	Delivered	Reduced	Demonstrated

Power Writing Examples

The following are examples of how power writing can improve the wording and general impact of a résumé. Both *wrong* and *right* examples are provided so that you can directly compare them. Note how the power writing rules, described earlier, are used to increase résumé effectiveness.

Wrong

I reported to the Plant Manager. I was responsible for the maintenance, engineering and procurement departments, and managed a total of 150 hourly employees. I was also responsible for managing the plant's stockroom and being sure that we didn't run out of spare parts.

Right

Reported directly to Plant Manager of this 2,000-employee paper manufacturing plant. Managed the maintenance, engineering and procurement functions (150 employees, $12 million budget). Directed $35 million capital expansion project which doubled plant production and reduced operating costs by 10%. Installed computerized spare parts system, reducing spare parts inventory by 25% ($1.3 million annual savings).

Wrong

I reported to the Director of Administrative Personnel. I was responsible for managing the compensation, benefits, employment and training functions. My major accomplishments included the installation of human resources computer system and new executive bonus program. I also managed the organization effectiveness function and contributed to the increased effectiveness of the corporate distribution function through use of modern organization effectiveness techniques.

Right

Reported to Director of Administrative Personnel of this Fortune 100 personal care and cleaning products company. Managed compensation, benefits, employment, organization effectiveness and training functions (35 employees, $12.6 million budget). Installed human resources computer system, reducing H.R. staff by 10% (annual savings $320 thousand). Lead O.E. effort that reduced corporate distribution operating costs by $48 million annually.

As can be seen from these examples, power writing can substantially improve the overall impact of the employment résumé. As you begin the actual résumé writing process, you will want to refer back to this chapter frequently, both for biographical data as well as writing techniques. Learning these power writing skills in advance should give you a head start in writing an orderly and hard-hitting résumé.

5

Résumé Style —
Picking the Right One

Most employment authorities would agree that there are essentially only two résumé formats that are worth your consideration—the chronological and the functional. Combined, they probably account for 80 to 85 percent of all résumés received by employers. Having to contend with just these two popular formats will make the selection process a lot simpler than some would have you think.

There is, perhaps, one major exception to this simple choice. In the case of those seeking employment in professions requiring a high level of creativity (i.e., artists or designers) there may be some benefit to a more inventive, unique approach. This book, however, does not attempt to deal with exceptional cases such as these. To do so would benefit only a very small portion of the work-eligible population, and create confusion at a time when understanding and clarity of mission are essential to effective résumé preparation.

BEWARE OF CHARLATANS

Unfortunately for the job seeker, and would-be résumé writer, there is a proliferation of bad advice on the subject of résumé preparation. It seems that the world abounds with self-proclaimed experts on this subject, and they are all too willing to share their misinformation with any unsuspecting soul who is willing to listen to their bogus counsel.

I am always amazed by the *credentials* of these quasi-experts, many of whom have little or no relevant employment experience. Unfortunately, because of their educational background, standing in the community, business position, or other tangible evidence of success, it is assumed by the unwary job hunter that these persons are truly knowledgeable about the subject of professional résumé preparation. Frequently, nothing could be further from the truth! This unfavorable counsel is perpetuated by the fact that many of these well-intentioned amateurs truly believe in the advice they are prescribing to their unwitting audience.

Regrettably, résumé preparation is one of those topics, like politics or religion, that practically everyone feels they know something about. Just ask, and you are bound to get an earful of guidance—most of it bad. If you are tempted to ask others for advice on this subject, or are about to buy a book on the subject, I have one admonition—*consider the source!*

Would you go to your barber for accounting suggestions? Your car dealer for real estate tips? Your attorney for spiritual help? Of course you wouldn't! Then why entrust a novice with something as important as preparation of your employment résumé? After all, the quality of your résumé could have significant impact on your current job hunting prospects, as well as your entire career. Why not be sure, then, that the person who advises you in this area is someone who is qualified to do so.

Here are some recommended questions to consider to be sure that you are dealing with a knowledgeable source:

1. How much actual employment experience has this person had?

2. How many actual persons has this individual been responsible for hiring? A few? Several hundred?

3. Has this person been responsible for hiring only into a narrowly-defined functional specialty (e.g., accounting, law, engineering, etc.); or has the employment experience spanned a wide range of functional disciplines?

4. Has this person's hiring experience been limited to only certain levels within the hiring organization (e.g., college entry level, professional level, middle management, top management, etc.), or has it transcended all organizational levels?

5. Importantly, how much résumé reading has this person actually done? Does he/she read all or most of the résumés, or are the bulk of these read by someone else?

6. Is this the person who, having read the résumé, makes the preliminary decision on which persons to invite in for interviews, or is this the person who merely reviews the résumés of those finalists whose résumés have been prescreened by someone else?

7. Is this person a *résumé expert* simply by virtue of the fact that he/she is now currently employed in the outplacement consulting business; or is this a person with significant, firsthand employment experience?

Yes, there are many impostors and would-be authorities in the business of dispensing résumé advice. Yours becomes the challenge of distinguishing between the seasoned expert and the well-intentioned novice. Hopefully, the questions I have posed will provide you with the necessary ammunition to draw a clear distinction.

A NARROW CHOICE

The market is saturated with a wide range of recommended résumé styles. Perhaps the assortment of formats is no less varied than the credentials of those who proffer them. There are those who advocate the analytical résumé, those who advocate the narrative résumé, the Harvard résumé, the creative résumé, the accomplishment résumé. The list of formats can go on and on.

But what about the proponents themselves? What basis do they have for their recommendations? Have they ever been in situations that allowed the opportunity to make firsthand observations about what really works and what doesn't? Unfortunately, were the truth known, many of these so-called experts have had little or no employment experience and, therefore, have little or no realistic, professional basis for their counsel. The net effect is a market with an excess of ill-founded, ill-conceived advice on résumé format; and a great deal of confusion and frustration among job hunters who are in search of the plain and simple truth.

WHAT THE EXPERTS RECOMMEND

Review of current literature on the subject of résumés reveals that experienced employment professionals are basically in agreement concerning acceptable résumé format. Depending upon the job seeker's particular circumstances, these experts unanimously agree that there are essentially only two recommended, acceptable choices. These are:

1. The chronological format
2. The functional format

Unlike the inexperienced counselors, seasoned employment professionals *do not recommend the use of unique or unconventional résumé styles.* By contrast, some tyros would have you believe that such uniqueness will set you apart from the masses, and the prospective employer will single you out for your brilliance and creative genius. "Nonsense," say the employment professionals. "Such advice will only expose you for the gullible sap that you really are and guarantee that your résumé will go forth into the endlessness of eternal oblivion."

In a more serious vein, use of an unconventional format may suggest one or more of the following to the professional:

1. The applicant is ignorant of proper résumé protocol.

2. The applicant lacks knowledge of commonly accepted business practice.

3. The applicant resists conformity, resents authority, and may therefore be a malcontent.

4. The applicant is a lone wolf, not a team player.

5. The applicant lacks good business judgment.

6. The applicant lacks good taste.

Conversely, use of a proper résumé format can suggest just the opposite:

1. The applicant is knowledgeable of proper résumé protocol.

2. The applicant is knowledgeable of commonly accepted business practice.

3. The applicant respects conventional authority and is well-adjusted.

4. The applicant is likely cooperative and a good team player.

5. The applicant exercises good business judgment.

6. The applicant demonstrates sound judgment and good taste.

Thus, most employment experts would agree that there are really only two viable résumé choices—the chronological format and the functional format. Use of any other style is to flirt with probable résumé failure. At best, you will likely lose résumé effectiveness and generally detract from your employment candidacy. At worst, you could kill your employment campaign before it even gets started.

Why take this chance when you can substantially improve your overall job search effectiveness through use of a proven, acceptable résumé style?

Let's now examine these two recommended styles. In doing so, consider the following questions:

Chronological Format

1. What is the chronological résumé?
2. What does it look like?
3. What are its advantages?
4. What are its disadvantages?
5. When should it be used?
6. When should it be avoided?

Functional Format

1. What is the functional résumé?
2. What does it look like?
3. What are its advantages?
4. What are its disadvantages?
5. When should it be used?
6. When should it be avoided?

THE CHRONOLOGICAL FORMAT

Take a moment to review the sample chronological résumé on page 67. What makes this a chronological format is the fact that the *Work History* section lists the positions held in a chronological sequence, starting with the most recent and working back to the individual's first professional job. So, technically, this particular format is really a *reverse chronological résumé*, and some prefer this terminology since it is more accurately descriptive. (For the sake of continuity, this book will use only *chronological résumé* in its reference to this format.)

The chronological résumé is by far the most popular and widely used résumé format. It probably represents a good 60 to 65 percent of all résumés received by employers. Without a doubt, it is the résumé style most preferred by seasoned employment professionals. With few exceptions, which are carefully explained later, I strongly recommend the use of this particular format above all others.

Advantages of Chronological Format

There are some very good reasons to choose the chronological résumé. These are as follows:

1. Since it is the most commonly used, it is the format with which employers are most familiar and feel the most comfortable.

2. The chronological format provides for a logical, easy-to-read flow with point-to-point continuity from one employment position and employer to the next.

3. This same logical flow makes it one of the easiest résumés to prepare.

4. This format allows the job hunter to emphasize career growth and progression (where he/she has experienced such)—two factors viewed favorably by most employers.

5. Likewise, this format serves to highlight continuity of employment (employer/job stability) and career continuity— both considered desirable factors by most employers.

6. This format also serves to highlight names of past employers, which can be advantageous where some or all of these are well-known, prestigious companies.

Disadvantages of Chronological Format

Although by far the most preferred résumé style, the chronological format is not without its disadvantages. And, there are certain circumstances which may dictate that it not be used at all. Possible disadvantages include:

1. This format can serve to highlight obvious employment handicaps, including:

   a. Job hopping

   b. Employment gaps

   c. Underemployment

   d. Lack of career progress

   e. Little or no related experience

   f. Age

2. Tends to draw attention to career progression, rather than to specific personal or functional strengths.

3. Tends to highlight most recent experience, when, in fact, certain earlier experiences may be more relevant to current job objective.

4. Tends to short-change certain key accomplishments, when these occurred earlier in the career.

When to Use Chronological Format

The following are provided as guidelines for determining when to use the chronological format:

1. This format is strongly recommended when all of the following factors exist:

    a. Reasonable/good career continuity.

    b. Reasonable/good career progression.

    c. Reasonable/good job stability.

    (You may want to think carefully about using the functional format instead, if any of these factors rank at the poor level.)

2. Where recent employment history is related to/supportive of current job objective.

3. Where overall employment experience is related to/supportive of current job hunting objective.

When Not to Use Chronological Format

There are times when the chronological résumé may not be appropriate to achieve maximum effectiveness. The following guidelines are provided to assist you in making this determination:

1. This format is not recommended when one or more of the following apply:

    a. Poor career continuity (i.e., there have been several changes in career direction).

     b. Little or no career progression (i.e., career has stagnated and there have been no promotions or advancement over an extended time period).

     c. Poor record of employment stability (i.e., four or more employers in last ten years; seven or more employers during professional career).

2. This format is generally inappropriate when recent employment history is unrelated to current job objective (unless such unrelated employment was of relatively short duration and was immediately preceded by relevant work experience).

3. The chronological format is also not indicated when there is little or no related work experience (i.e., a career change).

4. This résumé style would be inappropriate where there have been significant or frequent gaps in employment (i.e., unemployed for more than one year in last ten years; unemployed two or more times in the last five years).

5. The chronological format is not normally recommended when there has been an extended period of underemployment immediately prior to the job search (i.e., a significant reduction in job scope, level, and responsibility that has lasted one year or more).

6. This format is less than ideal when earlier employment experience is clearly more relevant to the current job target than are positions held in the recent past.

7. This style résumé may be less appropriate when relevant key accomplishments occurred earlier in the career.

THE FUNCTIONAL FORMAT

Take a moment to review the sample functional résumé on page 69. The functional résumé, as you will notice, highlights the employment candidate's background and accomplishments under broad functional categories. Categories chosen for emphasis are normally functional areas (i.e., cost accounting, market research, labor relations, finance, sales management, etc.). In each case, selected major accomplishments and results are then delineated under these key functional headings. Normally, these functions are listed in descending order based upon their relevance to the current job hunting objective. Thus, the most pertinent factors are listed first, with less germane points falling further down in the listing.

The functional résumé format is the second most popular résumé and represents an estimated 20 to 25 percent of all résumés received by employers. Although popular among job seekers, the functional format is far less popular with employers and with good reason. It is strongly recommended, therefore, that this résumé style not be used by you unless absolutely necessary. The rule of thumb is, *When in doubt, use the chronological format.* Let's take a look at the advantages and disadvantages of the functional résumé format.

Advantages of Functional Format

With the exception of the chronological résumé format, there are some good reasons to prefer the functional format over other less conventional styles. Key advantages of this format are as follows:

1. Since it is the second most commonly used, it is a format with which most employers are familiar and feel somewhat comfortable.

2. This format allows you to highlight the most relevant, job-related aspects of your background (i.e., functional experience, skills, accomplishments, etc.) even though these key qualifications are more evident from positions held earlier in your career.

3. Since it is not chronologically constrained, this résumé style allows you the flexibility of listing your most apropos qualifications first, thus drawing maximum attention to them.

4. The functional résumé format provides the opportunity to de-emphasize, or otherwise camouflage, a multitude of undesirable information, such as:

   a. Lack of career progress

   b. Lack of career continuity

   c. Job hopping

   d. Lengthy/frequent unemployment

   e. Lack of required experience

   f. Lack of required education

   g. Age

5. A functional format, which emphasizes key skills and capabilities, may suggest to the employer that there is more than one job where your capabilities could be utilized.

Disadvantages of the Functional Format

With the preceding list of advantages, it may be hard to imagine that there are many disadvantages to using the functional résumé format. However, this format does have some very real disadvantages that can substantially outweigh the previously cited advantages. These disadvantages are the very same ones that cause most employers and employment professionals to strongly prefer and advocate the use of the chronological résumé format. It is because of these same handicaps that I encourage careful thought and analysis before deciding to use this format. Remember, *When in doubt, use the chronological format.*

Major disadvantages of the functional résumé format are as follows:

1. This format arouses immediate suspicion on the part of the employer. Most employers are keenly aware that it is the format most frequently used by applicants who have something to hide, such as:

   a. Lack of career progress

   b. Lack of career continuity

   c. Frequent changes of job/employer

   d. Lengthy/frequent unemployment

   e. Lack of required experience

   f. Lack of required education

   g. Age

   This elicits a negative attitude right from the beginning, and the employer commences résumé reading as if on a witch hunt—focusing attention on searching out the problem, rather than on the candidate's qualifications for the position.

2. This format is difficult to read and creates confusion. The lack of logical continuity and completeness leaves the employer guessing about certain key factors important to the employment decision-making process. This leaves the employer with only one option—to call the candidate for clarification. Busy employment professionals won't even bother; they just move on to the next candidate's résumé.

3. The functional format can frustrate the employer. Since there is no linkage provided between specific positions held, and functional experience and results, the employer becomes easily thwarted in his or her attempt to make these connections. This sets off a negative, rather than a positive, attitude toward the job applicant.

4. Generally, this format is more difficult to prepare when compared to the chronological résumé format, where there is a more logical continuity of thought.

When to Use the Functional Format

Considering the disadvantages, you may be somewhat confused about when the functional format should be chosen over the chronological. Hopefully, you will find the following guidelines helpful when making this determination.

The functional résumé format should be used when:

1. There is some major, negative information that, if highlighted or disclosed, would almost certainly preclude further consideration of your employment candidacy. Examples of such *knock-out factors* are:

   a. Major career stagnation (i.e., no promotions or expansion of job responsibilities in last six years).

   b. Obvious lack of career continuity (i.e., frequent, continuous changes in career direction).

   c. Frequent changes of jobs/employers (i.e., four employers in ten years, seven or more employers during career, three or more recent jobs averaging less than two years duration, or, three or more jobs during career that were less than one year duration).

   d. Lengthy or frequent periods of unemployment (i.e., unemployed for more than one year in last ten years, two or more periods of at least yearlong unemployment, or, one period of two-year unemployment).

   e. Lack of critical experience considered essential to position.

   f. Lack of required education (unless there is sufficient relevant experience to offset this requirement).

2. When critical skills and capabilities would not be sufficiently evident from use of a standard chronological format (i.e.,

skills/capabilities were acquired through life experiences other than professional career employment).

3. When recent employment history is totally unrelated, or only distantly related, to current job objective, and earlier work experience is clearly more relevant.

4. When there has been a period of substantial underemployment (i.e., a significant reduction in job scope, level or responsibility) that has lasted for more than one year. (Note: Dependent upon the magnitude and duration of this reduction, it may still be advisable to use the chronological format, simply providing a brief description of this lesser position.)

5. When your career objective is not clearly defined and you wish to stress your overall skills and capabilities so that the employer might consider your qualifications for several areas. (Note: This is a very ineffective way to go to market, and substantially reduces the probability of a successful job hunting campaign.)

When Not to Use the Functional Format

It should be clear, from previous discussion, that the functional résumé format should not be used under these circumstances:

1. When there has been reasonable/good career progression.

2. When there has been reasonable/good career continuity (as well as career progression).

3. Where there has been a reasonable/good history of employment stability (provided such stability is coupled with reasonable/good career progression and career continuity).

4. Where career history is void of lengthy or frequent periods of unemployment (and items 1, 2, and 3 are also satisfactory).

5. Where critical work experience requirements (as well as items 1 through 4) are satisfied.

GENERAL OBSERVATIONS

As you can see from this discussion, selection of a proper résumé format is not a cut-and-dried decision. It requires some careful thought and consideration if you are going to select the format that will be most beneficial to you.

It is clear, however, that the disadvantages of using the functional résumé format, in the great majority of cases, outweigh those of the standard chronological format. At the risk of sounding like a broken record, the rule of thumb is, *when in doubt, use the chronological format.*

A WORD ABOUT RÉSUMÉ APPEARANCE

Putting the subject of résumé format aside, it is worthwhile to understand that the general appearance of the employment résumé is very important to the job hunting campaign. Think of the résumé as an extension of you. If it is neat, crisp, and well-organized, it will suggest to the employer that you are someone who is careful and concerned about the quality of your work. A sloppy, disorganized résumé, conversely, will create an unfavorable impression with prospective employers and greatly hinder, if not ruin, your employment efforts. It is imperative, therefore, that you be attentive to the general appearance of your résumé document, and that you take the necessary steps to make a favorable impression.

Here are some suggestions to improve the physical appearance and, therefore, the overall effectiveness of your résumé:

1. Use a high quality bond paper in either white or buff.

2. Carefully proofread and edit to ensure proper spelling, grammar, punctuation, and comprehension. (If necessary, seek help from a professional.)

3. Have your résumé professionally typed. At a cost of only a few dollars a page, you can hardly afford not to. This is a minor investment considering your entire career is at stake.

4. Have your typist advise you on proper style type. Avoid unusual or unique typefaces.

5. Make effective use of highlighting (bold type) and underlining to facilitate ease of reading and appropriate topical emphasis. (Note the sample résumés in this book for proper use of both, and tailor your résumé accordingly.)

6. Avoid ragged or uneven margins. Use of right margin justification by your typist will greatly enhance the appearance.

7. Make sure that final copy is neat, well-spaced, uncluttered and easy to read.

8. Final printing should be done by a professional printer using quality photo-offset printing equipment.

Although all of this may seem like basic advice, it is surprising what a high percentage of résumés don't meet these simple standards. What a shame, when it is so easy to improve the general appearance and overall effectiveness of this vital document. The extra effort can have substantial payoff for your job hunting campaign.

Since we have now completed a fairly indepth discussion concerning résumé format and appearance (and you have likely made the choice between using a chronological or a functional résumé format), we can now move on to actual résumé preparation. The next two chapters show how to effectively prepare these two formats. Several examples of each of these styles are also provided. Chapter 6 deals with the chronological format; Chapter 7 covers the functional format. Choose the appropriate chapter and proceed with actual preparation of your résumé document.

DAVID B. SAMPSON
325 Smithbridge Road
Old Forge, Pennsylvania 19872

Phone: (215) 872-8725

OBJECTIVE: Senior level management position in financial planning.

EDUCATION: M.B.A., University of Chicago, 1975
Major: Finance
Grade Point Average: 3.8/4.0
Class Rank: 8/165
Brasston Fellowship, 1973-1975

B.A., University of Wisconsin, 1973
Major: Business Administration
Grade Point Average: 4.0/4.0
Summa Cum Laude

WORK HISTORY:

1980 to Present <u>STARDAN MANUFACTURING, INC. (CORPORATE OFFICES)</u>

<u>Chief Financial Officer</u> (1985 to Present)
Report to the President of this Fortune 200 manufacturer of industrial valves and fittings (annual sales $3.8 billion). Functional accountabilities include business development, financial planning, finance, accounting and management information services. Manage 325 employee staff, $22 million budget, $2.7 billion corporate debt portfolio. Major contributions include: ten year financing of major $1.6 billion capital program at 1% below prime rate, successful acquisition of $80 million specialty valve manufacturer (first year net return 14%), successful installation & start-up of $5 million order tracking & invoicing computer system (annual savings $2.7 million).

<u>Director of Strategic Planning</u> (1983-1985)
Reported to Chief Financial Officer, with responsibility for business development and strategic planning (28 professionals, $1.6 billion budget). Directed development of first believable, five-year strategic planning computer model (60% timesaving on annual planning cycle). Directed acquisition studies on 18 candidates. Successfully completed 4 acquisitions totalling $185 million.

Résumé—Chronological

1975 to 1980   BARRINGTON CORPORATION (CORPORATE OFFICES)

Senior Financial Planner (1978-1980)
Reported to Director of Financial Planning of
$1.7 billion manufacturer of printed circuit
boards. Developed financial planning strategy
to fund annual capital requirements of $100 to
$125 million. Successfully negotiated $45
million loan for French affiliate at very
favorable rate and term.

Financial Planner (1976-1978)
Reported to Director of Financial Planning.
Planned funding strategy for an $85 million
capital expansion program.

Financial Analyst (1975-1976)
Reported to a Senior Financial Planner.
Responsible for determination of capital
funding requirements for various capital
projects.

PERSONAL: Married, 1 Child
                   U.S. Citizen
                   Excellent Health

REFERENCES: Excellent references furnished upon request.

Résumé—Chronological (Continued)

DAVID B. SAMPSON
325 Smithbridge Road
Old Forge, Pennsylvania 19872

Phone: (215) 872-8725

SUMMARY: Seasoned financial executive with 12 years
progressive management experience in all major
financial functions: finance, financial planning,
financial analysis, business development,
accounting and management information services.
Excellent record of advancement and increased
responsibility. A strong contributor to bottom
line results.

MAJOR ACCOMPLISHMENTS:

Financial Planning

-Directed all financial functions for Fortune 200
 manufacturing company (annual sales $3.8 billion).
-Directed long and short-term planning for $2.7
 billion corporate debt portfolio.
-Developed long-term financial planning computer
 model to forecast five-year capital requirements
 to within plus or minus 5%.
-Planned capital funding strategy for annual
 capital requirements of $100 to $125 million.

Finance

-Directed all financing, short and long-term, of
 $2.7 billion corporate debt portfolio.
-Financed major $1.6 billion capital program at 1%
 below prime rate.
-Financed $80 million acquisition with net return
 of 14% in first year.
-Negotiated all financing for 5 acquisitions
 (capital requirements totalling $350 million)
 with very favorable terms and rates.

Acquisitions

-Directed the analyses, negotiations and
 successful acquisition of 5 companies.
-Directed acquisition analysis and corporate
 recommendations on 18 candidates in 2 years.

Résumé—Functional

WORK HISTORY:

1980 to Pres.	<u>Stardan Manufacturing, Inc. (Corporate Offices)</u> Chief Financial Officer (1985 to Present) Director of Strategic Planning (1980-1985)
1975 to 1980	<u>Barrington Corporation (Corporate Offices)</u> Senior Financial Planner (1978-1980) Financial Planner (1976-1978) Financial Analyst (1975-1976)

EDUCATION:

M.B.A., University of Chicago, 1975
Major: Finance
Grade Point Average: 3.8/4.0
Class Rank: 8/165
Brasston Fellowship, 1973-1975

B.A., University of Wisconsin, 1973
Major: Business Administration
Grade Point Average: 4.0/4.0
Summa Cum Laude

PERSONAL:

Age 35
Married, 1 Child
U.S. Citizen
Excellent Health

REFERENCES: Excellent references furnished upon request.

Résumé—Functional (Continued)

6

Preparing the Chronological Résumé

This chapter will deal with preparation of the chronological résumé format. It is intended to walk you through each major component of the résumé with appropriate instructions. I will attempt to answer three basic questions as each résumé section is discussed. These questions are:

1. How should the section be written?
2. What should it contain?
3. What should be excluded?

SOME GENERAL OBSERVATIONS

Before you get started with this chapter and the preparation of your own résumé, I suggest that you take a few minutes to carefully study the several résumé samples contained at the end of the Chapter. There are several general observations that need to be made concerning the overall appearance of the résumé. They are:

1. Note that the candidate's name, and all major sectional headings (objective, education, work history, personal and references) are printed in capital letters, bold type and underlined. This serves to highlight these key areas, provides for ease of reading and facilitates the quick location of key information.

2. Note the positioning of dates in the Work History section of the résumé. Dates representing the total period of employment with each employer are positioned at the left hand margin. On the other hand, employment dates for each position held with these employers are shown in brackets to the right of their respective title. Visually separating the dates in this fashion avoids confusion concerning which positions were held with which employers. This also draws attention to employment stability rather than the perception of job hopping, which can happen when both the employer and position dates are listed together in the same column at the left margin of the résumé.

3. Note that all position titles are underlined and that the initial letters of each word in these titles is capitalized. This has the effect of visually subordinating the position title to the name of the employer, further reinforcing the impression of employment stability. It is also aesthetically pleasing and improves résumé readability.

4. Note the use of spacing throughout the résumé. Double spacing is used to separate each discrete segment to create readable units. Proper spacing enhances résumé appearance and readability, and makes locating specific topics easy.

5. Note the neatness and alignment of both margins and tabs. You will also notice that the left margin of all text material contained under each major section, is completely aligned. Right margins have been justified, eliminating the ragged effect. This overall

alignment adds substantially to the document's neat, crisp countenance and creates a very favorable impression.

6. Where possible, all text for each major résumé section should appear on the same page. This also improves the look and readability. Depending on the length and positioning of the text, this may not be possible without either cramming too much text against the bottom of the page, or leaving an abnormal amount of space. Use your best judgment.

RÉSUMÉ COMPONENTS

The basic components of the chronological résumé are:

1. Heading
2. Objective
3. Education
4. Work history
5. Military service
6. Personal
7. References

Although these sections are standard, and included in all chronological résumé formats, there are also some discretionary or optional components, which may or may not be included. In certain circumstances, it is recommended that these optional sections be included, and in other circumstances, it is specifically recommended that they be excluded. These discretionary components are:

1. Professional certification
2. Professional affiliations

3. Publications

4. Patents

5. Community service

6. Hobbies and activities

Guidelines concerning the use of these optional components can be found later in this chapter.

We will now proceed with a detailed description of each of the basic résumé components. In general, with few exceptions, they will be presented in the same sequence that they normally appear on the employment résumé. In this way, you can apply the advice given by simultaneously writing and developing each component of your own personal résumé. The cumulative effect of following this procedure will be the completion of your résumé by the time you have finished this chapter.

Don't forget all the background data that you formulated back in Chapter 4, *Résumé Writing—Advance Preparation.* You will want to draw information directly from the forms that you filled in. It is suggested that you take a moment to now review these forms.

HEADING

The résumé heading is fairly simple and straightforward. It consists of your name (in capital letters and bold print), address and home telephone.

Office telephone number can also be included; however, this may cause some employers to wonder why you are willing to accept calls concerning employment at your place of work. This may suggest that you have already been terminated and are in an outplacement mode, or you have recently been given notice. It is advisable, therefore, that you consider excluding the office phone number from your résumé, provided you can reasonably be reached at your home phone. For this reason, you may want to use an answering service or phone answering machine during your job hunting campaign.

OBJECTIVE

The objective portion of your résumé is important since it is the area of the résumé which is used to communicate both the level and type of position in which you would be interested. Without such a statement, employers are uncertain whether current openings would be a match for your position requirements. If you are a dead ringer for a current opening, in most cases lack of an objective statement would have little or no effect. In such cases, the employer will likely be calling you to discuss the position.

The problem comes when you would appear to have only some of the qualifications of the position. In such cases, lack of an objective statement could prove to be the one factor that knocks you out of contention for the position. Under the same circumstances, where there is a statement of objective that indicates an interest in the kind of work offered by the employer, this stated interest could well be the factor that swings the balance in your favor, and causes the employer to invite you for an employment interview.

It is essential that the statement of objective be properly worded. If the objective is too narrowly focused, it could have the effect of screening you out of opportunities in which you could well have an interest. On the other hand, an objective that is too broadly stated may suggest that you are vague or that you haven't given enough thought to your career. If you haven't given quality thought to something as important as your own career, how well will you handle the analytical and problem solving responsibilities of your job? This question is likely to be in the employer's mind, and could cast a shadow on your employment candidacy.

To further make this point, consider the following two objective statements:

1. Objective: Chief Financial Officer of major company with functional accountability for finance, strategic planning, business development, accounting and management information services.

2. Objective: Financial management position with major company.

The first objective statement is overly specific and might, therefore, have the effect of depriving the candidate of positions that may be of interest. For instance, use of the word *major* could cause the candidate, in this example, to be screened out by medium-sized and smaller companies. Likewise, the delineation of functional areas implies the candidate would only be interested in positions that included all of these functional areas. In such case, he/she might not be considered for a position as CFO for a company where the M.I.S. function did not report to this position.

The second objective statement, on the other hand, is stated so broadly that it is practically meaningless. Prospective employers are given no idea of the level and scope of the position sought. Without at least some parameters, it is difficult for the employer to determine whether a particular job opening is appropriate. Instead of taking the time to find out, the employer may just move on to the next résumé in the pile, in search of a clearly stated objective that suggests the candidate will be interested in the position currently open.

So, as you can see, a well-stated objective is a vital element of the résumé. Review some of the objective statements in the sample résumés found at the end of this chapter, and then try your hand at writing your own objective statement.

EDUCATION

Normally, the Education section of the résumé should contain the following components in this sequence:

1. Line 1: Degree awarded, school and date of graduation

2. Line 2: Major (and minor, if applicable)

3. Line 3: Grade point average (List if 3.0/4.0 or higher; exclude if less than 3.0/4.0)

4. Line 4: Class rank (List if top 10%; exclude if lower than top 10%)

5. Line 5: Scholarships/fellowships and years awarded

6. Line 6: Honors/awards and years awarded

With the passage of time, educational credentials take on decreasing meaning, and professional work experience and capabilities become increasingly more valid for the assessment of candidate qualifications. As a result, it is recommended that the more heavily-experienced persons consider positioning the Education section of the résumé immediately following the Work History section. Such positioning draws attention to experience and ability to contribute, rather than to age. In fact, in the case of those over age 50, it is advisable to list only degree and school, and exclude date of graduation. Why make it easy for an employer, who may potentially discriminate, to determine your age?

Age sensitivity is often dependent upon level in the organizational hierarchy. For example, an employer is less likely to be concerned about age when looking for a president than when in search of an entry level project engineer. Although equal opportunity laws have tempered the practice of age discrimination, we would be naive to think that such discrimination has been completely eliminated. So, if older, why highlight your graduation date by listing education near the beginning of your résumé and, thus, highlight your age?

The general rules of thumb concerning the positioning of the Education section of the résumé are:

Position education before work experience, if:

1. Your major and specific degree are related to/supportive of your job hunting objective.

2. You have graduated from a prestigious school (e.g., Harvard, Princeton, Yale, Columbia, Wharton, University of Chicago, Stamford, M.I.T.), and you have a relevant degree and major.

3. Your overall academic credentials are job target related and are also fairly impressive (e.g., graduate of well-known school with honors, recipient of prestigious scholarships/ fellowships, recipient of several honors/awards).

4. Your degree is recent and relevant to your job search objective. (The exception to this is if you are an older worker and the degree that you have just completed is at the undergraduate level.)

5. You are young, with limited experience, and are not concerned with emphasizing your age by showing date of graduation.

6. Your age is appropriate to your job level and you thus have no concern about revealing your age by showing graduation date.

7. In general, your educational credentials are supportive of your job search objective, so positioning Education before Work Experience enhances, rather than detracts from, your overall desirability as an employment candidate.

Position education after work experience, if:

1. Your degree and specific major are unrelated to, and therefore not supportive of, your job search objective.

2. You lack a graduate degree, and this is an absolute or preferred requirement for the position you seek.

3. You lack a formal degree, and this is normally required for the kind of position you want.

4. You graduated some time ago (usually 10 years or more), and you did not attend a well-known school.

5. Your age is incongruent with your job level (suggesting career stagnation or lack of promotability), and you do not wish to draw attention to your age early in the résumé by showing graduation date.

6. Your professional work history is generally more impressive and job target related than your educational credentials.

7. In general, your educational credentials are unrelated, unremarkable or in any other way detract from your desirability as an employment candidate for the position you seek.

The correct positioning of the Education section contributes to the overall success of the résumé. Sometimes it can be as important as the actual content of the section itself. Be sure, therefore, to give it careful consideration.

It is now suggested that you review the Education sections of some of the résumés at the end of this chapter. Then you can write the Education section of your own résumé.

WORK HISTORY

For the experienced person, the Work History section is probably the single most important part of the employment résumé. It is this portion, in particular, on which the employer focuses to determine whether you have the specific experience, knowledge, and skills to perform the duties of the position which the employer is attempting to fill. It is very important, therefore, that you invest adequate time and effort to do a particularly good job in describing this aspect of your background.

In preparing the Work History section, it is helpful to try to place yourself in the employer's shoes. What kind of information does the employer need in order to evaluate your background and qualifications? This is the same information that you will want to provide in the Work History section.

The first category of required information is that which relates to the employer. This includes:

1. Dates of employment

2. Name of employer

3. Location employed

The second category of information concerns the specific positions held. This includes:

1. Position title

2. Dates position held (from—to)

3. Reporting relationship (title of person to whom you reported)

4. Company description (size, products, services)

5. Size/scope of position (quantitative description of position— people and budgets managed, dollars impacted, etc.)

6. Functional responsibilities (functions for which you were responsible and titles of those who reported to you)

7. Major accomplishments/results (quantitative description of key results achieved—dollars saved, efficiencies gained, etc.)

From the exercises that you completed back in Chapter 4, most of this key information should already be at your fingertips. It is now a matter of organizing this data in a nice, logical flow for each of the positions that you have held. Remember to use the power writing skills that you also learned in Chapter 4, to dramatically improve the impact and effectiveness of this section of your résumé.

Take a few minutes to review the Work History sections of the résumés contained at the end of this chapter, and then proceed with writing a full description of each of the positions which you have held, using this format. Note the consistency of approach used in describing positions in the sample résumés. When describing each position held, topics are introduced in almost the identical sequence as listed above (i.e., reporting relationship, company description, size & scope of position, functional responsibilities and major accomplishments). Try to follow the same topical sequence and employ power writing techniques, when writing your own position descriptions. You should find that, in doing so, things will flow rather smoothly.

MILITARY SERVICE

If you are just being discharged from the military, or were recently discharged, and your military experience comprises the bulk of your employment history, you should include your military employment under the Work History portion of your résumé. In this case, you will want to provide a full description of your various assignments and accomplishments, much the same as you would in describing civilian experience in the same section.

Should your military service have occurred some time ago, and assuming this experience has little relevance to the position you are seeking, this service experience should be reported on the résumé under the heading Military Service, and should be treated fairly lightly. A format similar to the following should be used:

MILITARY SERVICE: United States Army, 1975–1976
                  2nd Battalion, Armoured Div.
                  First Lieutenant
                  Honorable Discharge, 6/2/76

PERSONAL

The Personal section of the résumé is very basic. This section normally includes:

Marital status

Number of children

Citizenship status

Health status

Although, as a basic rule, date of birth should be excluded from the résumé, there are two exceptions to this rule. The first exception is if you are, in fact, young (under age 30). The second is where you are particularly young for the organizational level of the position that you hold (e.g., a 32-year-old director, a 35-year-old vice-president, a 42-year-old president). In such cases, stating age could actually be advantageous since attaining these organizational levels at such an early age suggests that you are someone who has an unusually high level of drive and capability.

Women who are married and have children may not wish to include this information on the résumé. This is particularly true if applying for positions requiring extensive travel. Although protected from discrimination by federal law, these laws provide no absolute guarantee that you won't be discriminated against because of your marital status. Why raise a red flag and invite the possibility of such discrimination? The best advice is to simply leave marital and motherhood status off the résumé.

Likewise, persons who have a serious health problem, should also avoid mentioning this fact on their résumés. It is best, if necessary to do so, to handle this topic during face-to-face interviews.

REFERENCES

Never volunteer the names of references on the employment résumé. Simply indicate that you are willing to provide them at some future point. Providing references on the résumé is no longer a customary business practice, and may suggest to prospective employers that you are not current in your knowledge of acceptable business practices.

Additionally, one danger in listing references on the résumé is that the prospective employer may decide to contact these references before inviting you in for interviews. The slightest bit of negative input could serve to ruin your chances for an interview. Why take this risk? Instead, wait until you have had an opportunity to sell yourself in the employment interview. You will then have a much better chance of surviving a small bit of negative information picked up during the reference checking process.

As shown on the sample résumés at the end of this chapter, the Reference section should simply state that you are willing to provide proper references at the appropriate time. For this purpose, a statement such as the following is quite satisfactory: *Excellent references furnished upon request*. Or, you might simply state, *Excellent references available*.

This concludes the discussion on the basic components of the chronological résumé. Most often, use of these basic components (i.e., Heading, Objective, Education, Work History, Military Service, Personal, and References) is all that is necessary to ensure a complete and professional résumé. There are times, however, when consideration should be given to the additional résumé elements. These elements are: Professional Certification, Patents, Publications, Professional Affiliations, Community Service and Hobbies/Activities. A discussion of each of these discretionary or optional elements follows. Also provided are some basic guidelines for your use in deciding whether these should be included or excluded from your résumé.

PROFESSIONAL CERTIFICATION

Where you are employed in a professional capacity and your profession requires a certain body of technical knowledge and skill, it may be helpful to your employment campaign to be able to show that you have professional certification in your area of expertise. Citing such certification provides objective evidence to prospective employers that they are getting someone whose technical knowledge and skills are judged to be at an acceptable professional level. This is particularly important when the employer has no one on staff who has training in this particular specialty, and has no way of accessing the technical competence of employment candidates.

Professional Certification is normally positioned as a *stand alone* category on the résumé, and should immediately follow the Education section. Elements to be included in the Professional Certification section are: professional designation, name of certifying agency and date of certification. Some examples would be:

PROFESSIONAL
CERTIFICATION: Professional Engineer, New Jersey, May 12, 1982
                Certified Public Accountant, Maine, May 2,1976

PATENTS/PUBLICATIONS

Generally, if you are a scientist or engineer and have some patents and technical publications to your credit, this fact should be acknowledged on the résumé. This is also true of publications, if you are a writer. How much information you provide, and how specific you should be, depends directly upon how related this is to the type of position for which you are applying.

In those cases where patents and publications have little or no relevance to your job target, there is no point to listing them individually. This is also true if, in addition, these patents and publications are dated several years ago. In such case, it is suggested that they simply be shown under the single heading of Patents/Publications as follows:

PATENTS & PUBLICATIONS: 12 U.S. patents
24 Publications
2 Books

Although this information has little direct relationship to the absolute requirements of the position for which you are applying, it does suggest some positive things about you (i.e., you are creative, intelligent, technically knowledgeable, well-motivated, etc.). In most cases, this should prove beneficial to your overall image and employment efforts.

There is one exception, however. If you are a scientist or engineer with exceptionally strong technical credentials on the theoretical side, and are attempting to transition to a career requiring strong applied, hands-on skills, you may want to de-emphasize your theoretical skills by simply excluding any reference to patents and technical publications from your résumé. This is particularly true if you feel prospective employers might have a tendency to view you as too theoretical for the position for which you are applying.

Conversely, where patents and publications are relatively recent and are very much related to your job search target position, this information should clearly be included in the résumé. In those cases where there are only a few patents and publications, these can be listed under the single heading Patents/Publications. Where there are several items to be listed in each of these categories, it is suggested that you use two separate headings, Patents and Publications. These categories are usually positioned immediately after the Work History section. If the list of patents and publications is quite lengthy, exclude them from the body of the résumé, and instead list them on a separate page, entitled Patents and Publications.

When listing patents individually, you should include U.S. patent number, patent title, and date of issuance. Likewise, when listing publications individually, you should include title of the article, name of the publication in which article appeared, volume number, and publication date.

PROFESSIONAL AFFILIATIONS

Listing membership in professional associations is clearly an option when preparing an employment résumé. Simply having a membership in such organizations tells a prospective employer very little, if anything, about your technical skills and qualifications. It is merely testimony to the fact that you are professionally active. This certainly can't hurt, but it doesn't add anything meaningful to your qualifications.

The best criteria for deciding whether to include this category is space. If you can't add this information without unduly crowding other more important sections, or if it would warrant an additional page, I would recommend excluding these professional affiliations from your résumé. On the other hand, if there is sufficient space and the list of affiliations is both impressive and in some way related to your targeted position, I recommend you include them on the résumé under the heading, Professional Affiliations. This section should be positioned to follow Work History, Military Service, Patents or Publications, depending upon which of these categories was the last one listed on the résumé.

If you have held a leadership position in these organizations, it is suggested (assuming there is sufficient space on the résumé), that this information be spotlighted. The following is an example of how this might be done:

PROFESSIONAL		
AFFILIATIONS:	1968-Present	Employment Management Assoc.
		President (1986–1987)
		Vice President (1985–1986)
		Secretary (1984–1985)
	1980–1986	Amer. Soc. Personnel Admin.
		Vice President (1982–1983)
	1978–1980	Phila. Personnel Association

COMMUNITY SERVICE

Unless you are applying for a position where community service is directly related to your job objective, or where it can demonstrate leadership (e.g., you have been chairperson, president, or vice president) it is recommended that this section not be included in the employment résumé. Perhaps the only other exception to this is where it is known in advance that a specific employer is an advocate of community service, and strongly encourages its employees to get involved. In this case, there could be some reason to include this section in the résumé.

Should you include community activities in your résumé, it is suggested that a format similar to that for professional associations be used.

HOBBIES/ACTIVITIES

For the experienced person, the inclusion of hobbies and extracurricular activities adds little value to the résumé unless, of course, these hobbies and activities are directly related to your qualifications for the position you seek. Generally, however, there is little, if any, relevance and these items are best left off the résumé. Résumé space could, in all likelihood, be better used to describe other aspects of your background that speak more directly to your skills and qualifications for the position you are seeking.

There are some who would argue that hobbies and activities should be included since they can show that you are someone with broad, diverse interests. There is no absolute recommendation that can be made here, and it is best to temper your decision with common sense. If there is sufficient space, and your hobbies are varied and interesting, you may wish to include this category on your résumé. But, if you are short of space, or your list of hobbies and activities is small and lacks diversity, it might be best to exclude this information completely.

If you include a Hobbies/Activities section, position it just prior to the Personal section of your résumé. The generally accepted practice is to simply list hobbies and activities in the following manner:

<u>HOBBIES/ACTIVITIES</u>: Creative writing, antique restoration, skiing, skydiving, chess, and classical music.

Should any of these hobbies and activities suggest knowledge or skills that may be helpful to your employment candidacy, be sure to list these items first.

Thus ends the discussion of the chronological résumé. If you have followed along, preparing each section, step-by-step, you should now have a complete and effective employment résumé. The rest of this chapter consists of a number of sample chronological résumés for your review and reference.

ARTHUR J. WARRINGTON
1325 North Lake Road
Chicago, Illinois 19743

Phone: (516) 875-2861

OBJECTIVE: Senior level accounting position as Corporate or
Division Controller.

EDUCATION: M.B.A., Penn. State University, 1974
Major: Financial Management
Grade Point Average: 3.7/4.0

B.A., Penn. State University, 1972
Major: Accounting
Grade Point Average: 3.85/4.0

PROFESSIONAL
CERTIFICATION: C.P.A., Pennsylvania, 1978

WORK HISTORY:

1983 to Present   <u>NATIONAL BOTTLING COMPANY (CHICAGO, ILLINOIS)</u>

<u>Division Accounting Manager</u>
Report to the Division Manager with full accounting
and financial reporting responsibility for this
bottling division (5 company-owned franchises, $390
million sales, $150 million assets). Manage staff of
33 with functional accountability for financial
accounting, cost accounting, taxes and payroll.
Major accomplishments include: implementation of new
general ledger system, conversion to external
service bureau for payroll processing (annual
savings $250 thousand), reclassification of tax
asset base (annual savings $120 thousand).

1978-1983   <u>WALTER CHEMICALS, .INC. (CORNING, NEW YORK)</u>

<u>Corporate Accounting Manager</u> (1980-1983)
Reported to Director of Financial Accounting for
this $225 million manufacturer of chemical
specialties. Managed staff of 13 with functional
responsibility for financial reporting, payroll and
taxes. Key accomplishments included: installation of
on-line division computerized accounting system (cut
3 days off quarterly and year-end closings), major
department reorganization resulting in 25% headcount
reduction (annual savings $150 thousand), developed

Chronological Résumé—Accounting

89

new budget process based on the concept of zero based budgeting (annual savings of $1.7 million).

Manager of Cost Accounting (1978-1980)
Reported to Corporate Accounting Manager. Managed staff of 3 with corporate-wide accountability for all cost accounting activities. Developed new cost accounting procedures to gain better control over raw material inventories (cost savings $1.7 million).

1976-1978   PEAT, MARWICK, MITCHELL & CO. (PHILADELPHIA, PA)

Supervising Senior - Auditing   (1977-1978)
Staff Auditor   (1976-1977)

MILITARY SERVICE: United States Marine Corps., 1974-1976
3rd Battalion, Airborne Division
Captain
Honorable Discharge, May 15, 1976

PERSONAL: Married, 3 Children
U.S. Citizen
Excellent Health

REFERENCES: Excellent references furnished upon request.

Chronological Résumé—Accounting (Continued)

MARK L. RILEY
Arlington Towers
Apartment # 301
2235 Shively Blvd.
Baltimore, Maryland 17374

Phone: (301) 673-1863

OBJECTIVE: Senior Project Engineer with progressive company offering good opportunity for future advancement and professional growth.

EDUCATION: M.S., University of Maryland, 1982
Major: Electrical Engineering
Grade Point Average 3.6/4.0
Bolding Fellowship, 1981-1982

B.S., University of Wisconsin, 1981
Major: Electrical Engineering
Grade Point Average: 3.8/4.0
Cum Laude

WORK HISTORY:

1982 to Present <u>DELCO ELECTRONICS, INC (CORPORATE ENGINEERING)</u>

<u>Senior Project Engineer</u> (1985 to Present)
Report to Engineering Manager - Systems of this $875 million manufacturer of chemical control systems for papermaking wet-end applications. Engineer, install, start-up and debug complete computer control systems at customer sites in support of field sales. Provide on-call technical support to 13 existing customer sites in addition to handling 3 to 5 new installations annually (project budget $2 to $4 million). All projects have been delivered on schedule, with most at or below budget ($425 thousand savings in 2 years). Introduced unique interface design with System 2000, saving 25% on system installation costs.

<u>Project Engineer</u> (1982-1985)
Reported to Senior Project Engineer. Provided engineering support in the design, installation and start-up of System 2000 control system used for automated chemical control in papermaking processes.

PERSONAL: Age 28
Single
U.S. Citizen
Excellent Health

REFERENCES: Excellent references furnished upon request.

Chronological Résumé —Engineering

WHITNEY R. MURRAY
1825 Broadmeadow Blvd.
Wyomissing Hills, PA 19635

Phone: (215) 472-8953

OBJECTIVE: Chief Financial Officer with major corporation.

WORK HISTORY:

1980 to Present   EARTHSTAR INTERNATIONAL CORP. (CORP. OFFICES)

<u>V.P. & Chief Financial Officer</u> (1983 to Pres.)
Report to Senior Vice President of
Administration for this $5 billion, Fortune 150
manufacturer of military aircraft and satellite
equipment. Direct staff of 35 professionals
with responsibility for all short and long-term
financing to meet the present and future
capital requirements of the business. Annual
financing requirements average $500 to $600
million, with long-term debt portfolio valued
at $5.3 billion. Functions managed include
Corporate Finance, International Finance, Money
& Banking, Risk Management and Pension Funding.
Refinanced total long-term debt load at
substantially improved terms and improved rate
(annual savings $23 million). Improved credit
rating from AA to AAA, despite 25% increase in
domestic debt. Orchestrated aggressive investor
relations program with resultant increase in
stock prices from $28 to $86 per common share.

<u>Director of Financial Planning</u> (1980-1983)
Reported to Vice President & Chief Financial
Officer. Directed staff of 7 Financial Analysts
with full responsibility for forecasting and
planning the short and long-term capital
requirements of the business (average $500 to
$600 million per year). Developed five-year
financial planning computer model allowing
substantially improved accuracy in forecasting
capital requirements of international
affiliates (22 companies, 18 countries).
Planned and recommended restructuring of
intermediate term debt (potential savings $9.5
million).

Chronological Résumé—Finance

1975-1980   WOLVINGTON ELECTRONICS, INC. (CORP. OFFICES)

                 Senior Analyst, Corporate Finance (1978-1980)
                 Reported   to   Director   of   Corporate   Finance.
                 Responsible for analyzing and recommending alternate
                 financing methods and sources for wide range of
                 domestic   and   international   clients. Provided
                 consultation to top management of 3 business groups
                 in   the   development   of improved long-range capital
                 plans   and   forecasts. Developed first   believable
                 forecasting model for management use on IBM PC.
                 Provided   complete   financial   analysis, along   with
                 recommendations, on 6 potential acquisitions.

                 Financial Analyst, Corp. Finance (1975-1978)
                 Reported   to   Senior   Financial   Analyst   with
                 responsibility   to   assist   in   the   identification,
                 analysis   and   recommendation   of   a   wide   range of
                 business opportunities and financing options.

EDUCATION: M.B.A., Syracuse University, 1975
                 Major: Financial Planning

                 B.A., Bucknell University, 1973
                 Major: Accounting
                 Grade Point Average: 3.7/4.0
                 Dean's List, 1969-1973
                 Tarmac Scholarship, 1969-1973

PERSONAL: Age 35
                 Married, 3 Children
                 U.S. Citizen
                 Excellent Health

REFERENCES: Excellent references available upon request.

             Chronological Résumé—Finance (Continued)

MARY LYNN SEIGEL
Apartment 315
Cross Creek Apartments
825 Cross Creek Road
Stanfield, Connecticut 18746

Phone: (513) 876-2948

OBJECTIVE: Senior level human resources position with full responsibility for the corporate employment function.

WORK HISTORY:

1984 to Present   <u>WORTHINGTON ASSOCIATES, LTD. (NEW YORK, N.Y.)</u>

<u>Senior Consultant</u>
Report to Executive Vice President of this major international executive search consulting firm with 8 offices in the U.S. and 22 overseas. Responsible for development of new clients and generating revenue for the business by providing full range of executive search consulting services to client organizations. Generated $130 thousand of revenue in first year, $160 thousand in second year and successfully executed search assignments at the Board of Director, President, Vice President, Director, middle management and senior professional levels. Established strong rapport with clients leading to numerous compliments, repeat business and business referrals.

1970-1984   <u>CARLSON ELECTRONICS, INC. (WASHINGTON, D.C.)</u>

<u>Manager of Technical Employment</u> (1980-1984)
Reported to Director of Corporate Employment for this 20,000 employee, Fortune 200 manufacturer of printed circuit boards and electronic components (annual sales $2.9 billion). Managed the recruitment and employment of all technical and operations personnel for corporate office complex. Provided staff guidance and support to decentralized employment functions of 4 profit centers (20 plants). Hired 265 engineers, 18 engineering/operations managers and 7 executives (Director & Vice President level). Reduced interview to offer ratio from 8:1 to 2:1 (a 400% improvement) and offer to hire ratio from 3:1 to 1.5:1 (a 200% improvement).

Chronological Résumé—Human Resources

<u>Div. Mgr.- H.R. & Employment Svcs.</u>(1976-1980)
Reported to Director of Human Resources.
Responsible for all levels of salaried
recruiting and employment for this 1200
employee, high technology division involved in
precision coating of photographic films and
photoimaging equipment development. Complete
responsibility for most salaried personnel
services including: salary administration, job
evaluation (Hay System), benefits, human
resources planning and selection etc.

<u>Plant Personnel Manager</u> (1973-1976)
Reported to Plant Manager with responsibility
for the development, implementation and
administration of plant industrial relations
programs, policies and procedures for a 250
employee, non-union printed circuit
manufacturing plant. Managed a staff of 3 with
functional responsibility for employment,
employee relations, wage and salary
administration, training, benefits, safety and
security, medical, communications, public
relations etc.

<u>Personnel Assistant</u> (1970-1973)
Entry personnel position in a 2500 employee
electronic components manufacturing plant.
Reported to Plant Personnel Manager with
responsibility for providing assistance across
a wide range of human resources functions.

EDUCATION: B.A., Bucknell University, 1970
                    Major: Business Administration

PROFESSIONAL
AFFILIATIONS: 1975-Pres. Employment Management Association
                                   President   (1986)
                                   Vice President (1985)
                                   Secretary   (1984)
                    1980-1986 Nat. Assoc. Corp. & Prof. Recruit.
                    1972-1987 Nat. Assoc. Pers. Administrators
                    1980-1987 Human Resources Planning Society

PERSONAL: Married, 3 Children
                    U.S, Citizen
                    Excellent Health

REFERENCES: Excellent references furnished upon request.

Chronological Résumé—Human Resources (Continued)

95

KATHERINE A. LARSON
875 North Wallace Street
Troy, Michigan 18735

Phone: (513) 374-8926

OBJECTIVE: Senior corporate level position in marketing and sales management.

WORK HISTORY:

1980 to Present   BARTON EQUIPMENT COMPANY (CORPORATE OFFICES)

Vice President - Marketing & Sales (1983-Pres.)
Report to President of this Fortune 300, $1.9 billion manufacturer of earth moving, excavation and mining equipment. Direct marketing & sales organization of 125 employees with annual budget of $115 million. Functions managed include: Market Research, Market Planning, Market Development, Advertising and Field Sales. Increased sales by 25% in 2 years through introduction of new sales incentive plan combined with training sales force in effective "closing" techniques. Reorganized sales districts with subsequent reduction in headcount of 10% ($1/2 million savings). Successfully introduced new Huffy line in declining market (15 units sold in 6 months).

Director of Marketing & Sales (1980-1983)
Reported to Vice President - Marketing & Sales with functional responsibility for all marketing and sales functions (105 employees, $105 million budget). Established regional dealership network (25 key cities) to sell new Big Kat line to major highway contractors (attained 32% of market share in 3 years). Worked with R & D to redesign and reposition Mighty Mack line of miniature dozers for sale to residential developers. Sales tripled in two years ($25 to $75 million).

1976-1980   BULL DOG TRUCKS, INC. (WARREN, OHIO)

National Sales Manager
Reported to Vice President of Marketing of this $765 million manufacturer of light duty dump trucks sold to light commercial and residential developers. Managed 65 employee field sales force (annual budget $3.5 million). Revamped field sales organization, releasing and replacing 28 representatives and restructuring sales territories, resulting in 30% increase in

Chronological Résumé—Marketing & Sales

sales in one year. Increased Little Bull market share by 22% in 3 years. Increased Big Bull market share by 18% during same period.

1970-1976   RATHCHILD EQUIPMENT CO. (ERIE, PENNSYLVANIA)

<u>Senior Sales Representative</u> (1973-1976)
Reported to National Sales Manager of this regional distributor of street cleaning equipment (annual sale $85 million). Sold street cleaning equipment to municipalities in three state area (Pennsylvania, New York and Virginia). Increased territory sales by 300% in 3 years. Named "Salesperson of the Year" -- 1974, 1975 and 1976.

<u>Sales Representative</u> (1970-1973)
Reported to National Sales Manager. Sold street cleaning equipment to municipalities in eastern Pennsylvania and New York states.

<u>EDUCATION</u>:   B.A., Penn State University, 1970
Major: Business Administration
Varsity Field Hockey, 1966-1970

<u>PERSONAL</u>:   Married, 1 Child
U.S. Citizen
Excellent Health

<u>REFERENCES</u>:   Excellent references available.

Chronological Résumé—Marketing & Sales (Continued)

MARGARET R. TEMPLE
815 General Howe Road
East Chester, Pennsylvania 19385

Phone: (215) 420-7836

OBJECTIVE: Corprate vice presidential level position with full responsibility for material management functions corporate-wide.

EDUCATION: M.B.A., Harvard Business School, 1970
Major: Finance

B.S., Princeton University, 1968
Major: Industrial Engineering
Grade Point Average: 3.8/4.0
Ford Motor Scholarship, 1964-1968
General Foods Scholarship, 1967

WORK HISTORY:

1980 to Present   AMERICAN NATIONAL OIL COMPANY (HOUSTON, TEXAS)

Director - Traffic Planning
Report to Vice President of Distribution of this $8 billion, Houston-based oil exploration and production company. Manage multinational staff of 285 transportation professionals ($200 million budget) in the international transport of $1.9 billion crude and refined product annually. Develop and administer large volume contracts for air and ocean transportation, trucking, heavy lift movement, container leasing, container repair, household goods import/export , cargo documentation and customs brokerage. Senior advisor to Corporate Management on international transportation matters. Reduced transportation costs by $20 million (10%) in two years through implementation of new computerized planning system. Also cut transportation delivery times by 27% through improved loading techniques and better scheduling.

1975-1980   VICKSTON FOUNDRY COMPANY (WARREN, OHIO)

Director - Materials Management
Reported to Vice President Operations of this $180 million iron foundry. Functional responsibilities included Purchasing, Traffic , Stores and Raw Material Control. Managed staff of 65 with responsibility for annual purchases of $120 to $130 million and inventories of $25 million. Initiated raw material cost reduction

Chronological Résumé —Materials Management

projects totaling $3 million savings. Implemented sophisticated stores inventory control and accounting computer system at 4 plant sites ($3/4 million savings). Led development of computerized raw material cost optimization model resulting in $1/2 million cost savings per year.

1970-1975   BELLVILLE FOUNDRY, INC. (BELLVILLE, OHIO)

Manager - Operations Anal. & Plng. (1973-1975)
Reported to Director of Operations. Analyzed company operations, prepared business plans and monthly reports for corporate management. Coordinated capital expenditure, energy conservation, government price control reporting and cost reduction programs.

Manager - Production Planning (1970-1973)
Reported to Operations Manager with responsibility for forecasting, production planning, scheduling and inventory control systems.

PERSONAL: Age 39
Married, 1 Child
U.S. Citizen
Excellent Health

REFERENCES: Excellent references available upon request.

Chronological Résumé —Materials Management (Continued)

JEFFREY A. MORSE
125 East Lansing Street
Lansing, Michigan 17465

Phone: (318) 763-2959 - Work
       (318) 763-3887 - Home

OBJECTIVE:

Senior level operations management position with corporate-wide accountability for all manufacturing and related services.

WORK HISTORY:

1976 to Present

ENVIRONMENTAL SCIENCE, INC. (CORPORATE OFFICES)

Vice President of Manufacturing (1981 to Pres.) Report to President with total P&L responsibility for 5 manufacturing plants for this $575 million manufacturer of air and water pollution control equipment. Direct the activities of 6 person manufacturing staff, 5 plant managers, 436 salaried and 6,345 hourly employees with annual budget of $400 million. Implemented new "total quality" program, based upon statistical quality control concepts, resulting in 20% increase in productivity ($80 million savings) in two years. Directed participatory management work design efforts at two plant sites resulting in 12% headcount reduction ($9 million savings). Installed corporate-wide materials management inventory control system that reduced raw material inventories by 18% ($7.3 million).

ENVIRONMENTAL SCIENCE, INC. (WAKEFIELD PLANT)

Plant Manager (1976-1981) Reported to Vice President of Manufacturing with full P&L responsibility for this 1,600 employee fume incinerator manufacturing plant ($130 million annual production). Functions managed included manufacturing, distribution, engineering, maintenance, procurement, accounting and personnel. Organized and directed special joint union/management cost reduction task force which identified and implemented cost reduction opportunities resulting in a 10% ($11 million) reduction in overall manufacturing costs. Successfully started up metal fabrication assembly line beating both learning curve (by 4 months) and budget (by 14%) in first year. Awarded "Plant of the Year Award" for 1981, 1980, 1979 and 1977.

Chronological Résumé—Operations

1966-1976

<u>BORK AIR CONDITIONING, INC. (CORPORATE OFFICES)</u>

<u>Manager of Engineering</u> (1971-1976)
Reported to Vice President of Manufacturing.
Managed 85 employee Corporate Engineering
function for this $260 million manufacturer of
commercial and industrial air conditioners.
Directed engineering organization in all
capital project expansion programs to include
design, engineering, installation and start-up
of all metal fabrication and air conditioner
assembly facilities. Successfully engineered
and started up $320 million, 220,000 square
foot air conditioner fabrication and assembly
plant in Columbus, Ohio. Project completed on
time and $1.6 million under budget.
Successfully completed over $500 million in
capital projects in 5 years.

<u>BORK AIR CONDITIONING, INC. (TAMPA PLANT)</u>

<u>Department Manager - Fabrication</u> (1969-1971)
Managed 120 employee metal cabinet fabrication
operation with annual production valued at $85
million. Changed line layout and improved
production output by 13% ($9 million) in two
years.

<u>Project Engineer</u> (1966-1969)
Reported to Operations Manager. Responsible for
design, installation and start-up of various
capital projects in air conditioner fabrication
and assembly.

<u>EDUCATION</u>:   B.S., University of Michigan, 1966
                Major: Mechanical Engineering
                Grade Point Average: 3.6/4.0

<u>PERSONAL</u>:   Married, 3 Children
                U.S. Citizen
                Excellent Health

<u>REFERENCES</u>:   Excellent references available upon request.

Chronological Résumé—Operations (Continued)

101

LINDA B. DUKES
202 Fairfield Avenue
Atlanta, Georgia, 87264

Phone: (414) 326-1987

OBJECTIVE: Chief information officer or vice president of MIS for a large or medium-sized company.

WORK HISTORY:

1984 to Present   **COMPUTER SYSTEMS, INC.(CORPORATE OFFICES)**

Vice President - Information Resources
Report to President of this $50 million software development and marketing company. Functional accountability includes strategic planning, product development and marketing. Direct staff of 350 in the development and sale of specialized accounting and cost control software to hospitals throughout the U.S. and Canadian markets. Developed new IDMS based general ledger software product that captured 23% of the community hospital market in the Northeast Region. Led development of new Southern Region, with sales now exceeding $18 million. Developed and implemented highly successful site-based operating methodologies that have facilitated data conversion at customer sites.

1982-1984   **MONTGOMERY COUNTY (NORRISTOWN, PENNSYLVANIA)**

Director of Information Services
Reported to Vice President of Administration. Directed all information management in the county government including telecommunications (voice, data, video and radio) and data processing. Managed a staff of 225 and annual budget of $13 million. Reduced staff by 8% (annual savings $3/4 million) and simultaneously increased productivity by 10%. Led transition from traditional management system to a participatory, sociotechnical based system. Developed on-site personal computer training center.

1978-1982   **COMPUTER DATA CORPORATION (CORPORATE OFFICES)**

General Manager - Peripheral Systems
Reported to Director of Marketing. Responsible for developing market strategy for introduction of plug-compatible peripherals to IBM marketplace outside U.S. Directed 18 country

Chronological Résumé—MIS

marketing organization in the development of appropriate strategy for market introduction and oversaw initial market entry. Generated revenues of $38 million and net profits of $9 million in two years from date of market entry. Instituted reliability testing system to assure reliability of internationally shipped equipment.

1976-1978   PIMA COUNTY (TUCSON, ARIZONA)

Director of Data Processing
Reported to Vice President of Administration. Responsible for management of 40 person staff and $1.2 million budget in providing data processing services to all county departments. Substantially improved morale and quality of service provided by department through the use of participatory management concepts and techniques.

1970-1976   DARLINGTON CORPORATION (CORPORATE OFFICES)

Senior Systems Analyst (1974-1976)
Reported to Manager of MIS. Installed $2 million general ledger system. Project completed on time and within budget.

Systems Analyst (1970-1974)
Evaluated and recommended several software packages for various client applications.

EDUCATION: M.S., University of Virginia, 1970
Major: Computer Science
Grade Point Average: 3.6/4.0

B.S., West Chester University, 1968
Major: Computer Science

PERSONAL: Age 39
Married
U.S. Citizen
Excellent Health

REFERENCES: Excellent references available upon request.

Chronological Résumé—MIS (Continued)

7

Preparing the Functional Résumé

The functional résumé format has long been one of the more popular résumé formats. Second only to the chronological format, the functional résumé is the most widely-used résumé style, representing about 20 to 25 percent of all résumés received by employers. It deserves your consideration when deciding what résumé style will best represent your credentials.

As discussed in Chapter 5, Résumé Style—Picking the Right One, there are times when use of the functional résumé is clearly not in your best interest. If you have not already done so, it would behoove you to read Chapter 5 before arbitrarily choosing the functional format. In most instances, in fact, you will find that chronological résumé format will better serve your needs.

Perhaps the single greatest drawback to use of the functional résumé is that it is the style most frequently used when the employment candidate has something to hide. Typically, it is used to disguise such things as:

1. Lack of career progress

2. Lack of career continuity

3. Frequent changes of job/employer

4. Periods of lengthy or frequent unemployment

5. Lack of prerequisite experience for position

6. Lack of prerequisite education for position

7. Age

Seasoned employment professionals are immediately suspicious when they see a functional résumé. Instead of focusing on the candidate's credentials, therefore, there is a tendency to try to find out what it is that the candidate is concealing. This sets up some negative thoughts right from the start, which may cause the employer to shy away from your candidacy.

Before scaring you away from the functional résumé entirely, it is important to point out that there are times when the functional résumé is the preferred résumé format. Chapter 5 covers this topic in great detail and should be referred to before choosing which format you will use. After all, you want the best format working for you that you can get—the one that most effectively markets you and your background to prospective employers. Don't leave résumé format selection to chance, it's simply too important to your job hunting campaign.

OVERVIEW OF FUNCTIONAL FORMAT

The functional résumé, unlike the chronological résumé, which focuses on the chronology of positions held, focuses on the employment candidate's background and accomplishments under broad functional categories. Here the attempt is to choose those functional areas which are most related to the position sought, and then to cite specific experience and accomplishments related to each of these key functional categories. Functional categories chosen for highlighting are normally those thought to be important functional accountabilities of the position for which the job candidate is applying.

By choosing functional areas important to the target job, and citing evidence of your ability to achieve meaningful results, it is believed that the functional résumé format can be a fairly powerful tool. If well-prepared, such a presentation can showcase historical evidence of your overall qualifications and capabilities and will certainly get the employer's attention.

This same approach can be used to focus on job-related skills as well. In this case, you would simply select specific skills that are important to job performance and emphasize these skill areas instead of job functions. As with the function-based résumé, under each skill heading the candidate cites examples of specific results and accomplishments which demonstrate proficiency in these key skill areas. The skill-based résumé format is most frequently used by those candidates having little or no functional experience in the areas required by the position. Typically, this approach is used by recent graduates or persons having little or no job-related experience.

Clearly then, the key advantage of the functional résumé is that it permits the employment candidate to focus on key job functions or skills and to draw the employer's attention to his or her strengths in these important areas. The remainder of this chapter will be devoted to leading you through a step-by-step process for preparing an effective functional résumé.

RÉSUMÉ COMPONENTS

Review of the sample functional résumés at the end of this chapter will reveal that the functional résumé has six basic components as follow:

1. Summary

2. Major accomplishments

3. Work history

4. Education

5. Personal

6. References

Unlike the chronological résumé, the order in which these components are presented on the résumé does not vary. Instead, they are listed in the same order as they appear here. The reason for this is fairly logical. The emphasis of this format is on functional accomplishments and these must therefore be presented at the beginning of the résumé. To list education or work history before major accomplishments would take the focus away from these accomplishments and would, therefore, be self-defeating.

Beyond these basic components, as with the chronological résumé, there are some optional components which you may or may not wish to include. They are:

1. Professional certification

2. Professional affiliations

3. Publications

4. Patents

5. Community service

6. Hobbies/activities

For a thorough discussion of these optional areas, refer back to Chapter 6. The focus here will be on how to prepare the basic components of the functional résumé.

What follows is a detailed review of each basic component of the functional résumé. By following the instructions provided in each of these steps as we discuss them, you will end up with a well-prepared and effective functional résumé.

HEADING

Preparation of the résumé heading is simple and straightforward. Essentially, there are three elements to the résumé heading. They are:

1. Name

2. Address

3. Telephone number

Review of the sample résumés at the end of this chapter will reveal that all three parts of the heading are centered. In addition, there are three spaces separating the résumé heading from the rest of the text. You will also note that the candidate's name is printed in capital letters and bold type, causing it to stand out from the rest of the heading.

Although it is common practice to list home phone number in the résumé heading, there has long been a debate by résumé professionals whether the work phone number should also be included. Listing the work number may raise some questions on the part of prospective employers concerning why you will allow contact at your place of employment. Perhaps you have already been terminated by your current employer and are being allowed to conduct your job search from your employer's office? Perhaps you are expecting to be terminated shortly and really don't care if your employer discovers that you are looking for other employment? Perhaps you are a person who frequently uses company time to conduct personal business? These and other similar questions may enter the prospective employer's mind if you include your office phone number in the résumé heading. None of these reflects favorably on your employment candidacy.

Generally, it is recommended that the work phone number be excluded from the employment résumé. Prospective employers, who want to reach you can use the mail or can send a wire to your home address. In addition, they can call you at home during evening hours (a very common practice among employment professionals). If you are difficult to reach by phone, you might consider using the cover letter, which accompanies your résumé, to list the name and phone number of a trusted individual who can normally be reached during working hours.

Further review of the sample résumés contained in this chapter will show that the telephone number is separated from the rest of the heading by use of double spacing. This provides for ease of reading and fast location in the event the employer wishes to contact you.

SUMMARY

The intended purpose of the summary section of the résumé is to give the employer just enough information about you to compel reading of the balance of your résumé. This is normally done by conveying some idea of the depth and breadth of your experience and by also highlighting some of your key strengths in areas of likely interest to the prospective employer.

Review of the sample résumés at the end of this chapter will reveal that summary sections have some similarities. First, the initial sentence of each summary statement reports the writer's career or professional area, and cites the number of years of experience. The second sentence is normally used to market key job-related strengths. Finally, the third sentence is normally used to further convey the breadth of the candidate's experience. Alternately, this third sentence can be used to further market some unique skill or fact that would likely be perceived as valuable by the prospective employer.

The summary section of the résumé should be concise and to the point. It should not be a lengthy, rambling epistle. Component statements need not be written in complete sentences. Instead, they may be written as simple descriptive phrases that are intended to be hard-hitting and concise—much the same as the approach used in advertising. One simple rule to be used in accomplishing this is to begin each statement with an adjective followed by a noun. This will force you to be brief and to the point.

MAJOR ACCOMPLISHMENTS

When organizing this section of the résumé, it is best to start by mentally focusing on the target job you are seeking, and then asking yourself the following questions:

1. What are the key functional responsibilities of the target position?

2. How should these be ranked in order of their importance to the position?

3. In which of these functional areas do I have meaningful experience?

4. What have been my three or four major accomplishments in each of these functional areas?

Considerable time can be saved at this point by referring to the preliminary work already done by you in Chapter 4. By referring back to this chapter, it should be relatively easy for you to quickly identify your major accomplishments. Although they are arranged in chronological job sequence, it should be simple to classify them under the functional categories that you have chosen to highlight on your résumé.

If you have little or no relevant experience, as an alternate to this functional approach, you may wish to use a skills-based approach to the functional résumé. Should you elect to do this, you will need to answer the following questions:

1. What is the position I am seeking?

2. What are the key functional accountabilities of this target position?

3. What are the key skills necessary to successful performance of these functions?

4. Which of these skills have I acquired?

5. How have I used these skills and with what results?

In this case, instead of highlighting functional areas on the résumé, you will want to choose broad skill categories that are important to functional job performance. Under each of these broad skill categories, you should list major accomplishments or results that demonstrate your skill proficiency in each of these relevant skill categories.

When listing the functional or skill categories you wish to stress on your résumé, it is important that these categories be presented in order of priority. Those categories considered to be most important to the target position should be listed first, with least relevant category listed last.

Although this sequence is the most frequently recommended and used by functional résumé writers, there are times when the ordering of these categories should be based upon criteria other than just job-relatedness. In particular, where some of your accomplishments and results under one of these categories are clearly outstanding when compared to other functional or skill categories, such category should be listed first on the résumé with the others assuming a subordinate role. The logic that supports this sequencing is the old adage, *Lead with your strength*. All else being equal, however, it is best to arrange these categories in accordance with their importance to the target position, as suggested in the previous paragraph.

Review of the sample résumés contained in this chapter will show that each of the category headings chosen for emphasis should be underlined with the first letter of each word in caps. Additionally, to improve résumé aesthetics and overall readability, each category heading should be preceded and followed by double spacing.

In keeping with the power writing principles outlined in Chapter 4, each of the accomplishment statements listed under the functional categories should be started with a verb. This will force you to write brief, meaningful statements. Where possible, such result statements should contain quantitative information which provides the reader with some understanding of the magnitude of the result. This is particularly true if such results were of significant magnitude (e.g., a 40 percent increase in sales, a 25 percent reduction in costs, a 60 percent increase in productivity).

As with the functional (or skill) categories themselves, the statements of accomplishment listed under each of these categories should be listed in order of their importance to the overall functional accountability of the target position. Here again, however, where a particular accomplishment has significant more impact than others included under the same functional category, such accomplishment should be listed first, with the balance of results statements following. Once again, *Lead with your strength* applies.

WORK HISTORY

The work history section of the résumé should be organized in reverse chronological order. Start first with your current or most recent employer, and then go backwards in time to the first employer for whom you worked. The format followed here is similar to that used in the chronological résumé with the exception that no descriptions of positions are provided.

Review of the sample résumés at the end of this chapter will show the following consistent sequence:

1. Dates of employment with each individual employer are listed at the left hand margin.

2. Names and locations of the employers are then listed to the right of these employment dates. Both the name of the employer and location are underlined with the first letter in each word in both the employer's name and location printed in caps. (This provides for ease of readership.)

3. The title of each position held with a respective employer is then listed in reverse chronological order (i.e., most recent position held listed first). The first letter of each word in the job title is capitalized.

4. The dates of employment for each position held are listed in brackets to the right of the position. (This serves to avoid confusion concerning which positions were held with which employer and makes it perfectly clear that these dates are job-related.)

5. Note the use of spacing. Double spacing is used to separate employers, with single spacing used between titles of

positions held. (This serves to visually separate employers, thus providing for ease of reading.)

EDUCATION

As with the chronological résumé, the education section of the functional résumé should include the following information in the sequence shown:

1. Line 1: Degree awarded, school, and date of graduation

2. Line 2: Major (and minor, if applicable)

3. Line 3: Grade point average (List if 3.0/4.0 or higher; exclude if less than 3.0/4.0)

4. Line 4: Class rank (List if top 10%; exclude if lower than top 10%)

5. Line 5: Scholarships/fellowships and years awarded

6. Line 6: Honors/awards and years awarded

Although Education is generally positioned to follow the Work History section, it can be listed first if to do so would strengthen the overall impact of the résumé. The question you need to ask is, "Which category—Education or Work History—contains the most job-related and impressive credentials?" For the experienced person, the answer will most likely be Work History. For the person with little or no work experience, however, the answer could well be Education. When in doubt, the rule of thumb is to position Work History before Education. This is a functional résumé, after all, and the whole purpose is to draw attention to your functional credentials for the target position. This is usually defeated when Work History is positioned after Education.

PERSONAL

The Personal section of the functional résumé is fairly basic. This section normally includes:

Marital status

Number of children

Citizenship status

Health status

Although, customarily, age should be excluded from the résumé, there are two exceptions to this rule:

1. You are under age 30.
2. You are particularly young for the organizational level of the position which you hold (e.g., a 33-year-old director, a 36-year-old vice president, a 41-year-old president).

In these cases stating age or date of birth on the résumé can prove advantageous. Otherwise, leave it off!

Women who have children may not wish to include this information on their résumé. This is particularly true if applying for positions involving overnight or extensive travel. Although sex discrimination is illegal, you would be naive to think that some employers do not practice such discrimination. Why give them an opportunity to do so? The best advice is to exclude this information from your résumé and avoid the problem entirely.

Likewise, persons having chronic health problems should avoid showing this fact on their résumé. If revelation of your health problem is unavoidable, I suggest you save such for the interview discussion rather than to *red flag* it on your résumé, and potentially eliminate the very possibility of an employment interview.

REFERENCES

Never volunteer the names of references on the employment résumé. It is better to simply indicate that you are willing to provide this information at the appropriate time.

By listing actual references on the résumé, it is possible that you may preclude the possibility of an employment interview. An overly zealous employer may elect to check these references in advance of scheduling an on-site interview and may, in the process, discover the slightest bit of negative information. This could serve to squelch the possibility of a face-to-face interview, and the opportunity to present your side of the story.

Why take this chance? Instead, wait until you have had the opportunity to sell yourself in the interview. If you do a good job in the interview, the positive impression that you create could more than offset a small bit of negative information picked up by a prospective employer during the reference checking process.

As demonstrated in the sample résumés at the end of this chapter, the reference section of the résumé should convey a willingness to provide the prospective employer with the names of references at the appropriate time. Statements such as the following will do nicely:

1. Excellent references furnished upon request.
2. Excellent reference available.

ARTHUR J. WARRINGTON
1325 North Lake Road
Chicago, Illinois 19743

Phone: (516) 875-2861

SUMMARY: Seasoned accounting manager with 11 years experience in
business and public accounting. Broad general
accounting experience at the corporate, division and
manufacturing levels. Strong record of cost control and
savings contributions.

MAJOR ACCOMPLISHMENTS:

Corporate Accounting

-Directed corporate accounting function for $225
million chemical specialties manufacturer.
-Managed staff of 13 with functional accountability for
financial reporting, accounting, payroll and taxes.
-Installed on-line computerized accounting system
cutting 3 days off quarterly and year-end closings.
-Reduced department headcount by 25% through
reorganization.
-Installed zero based budgeting program resulting in
$1.7 million annual savings.

Division Accounting

-Directed division accounting function for $390 million
bottling operation (5 franchises, $150 million assets)
-Managed staff of 33 with functional accountability for
financial reporting, cost accounting tax and payroll.
-Implemented new computerized general ledger system.
-Converted to external service bureau payroll
processing ($1/4 million annual savings).
-Reclassified tax asset base ($120,000 annual savings).

Cost Accounting

-Managed corporate cost accounting department (staff
of 3).
-Developed inventory cost control system ($1.7 million
savings).
-Implemented new manufacturing cost standards resulting
in identification of source of major energy loss
($3/4 million annual cost savings).

Functional Résumé

WORK HISTORY:

1983 to Pres. <u>National Bottling Company (Chicago, Illinois)</u>
                Division Accounting Manager

1978 to 1983 <u>Walter Chemicals, Inc. (Corning, New York)</u>
                Corporate Accounting Manager   (1980-1983)
                Manager of Cost Accounting   (1978-1980)

1976 to 1978 <u>Peat, Marwick, Mitchell & Co. (Philadelphia, PA)</u>
                Supervising Senior - Auditing (1977-1978)
                Staff Auditor (1976-1977)

EDUCATION: M.B.A., Penn State University, 1976
                Major: Financial Management
                Grade Point Average: 3.7/4.0

                B.A., Penn State University, 1974
                Major: Accounting
                Grade Point Average: 3.85/4.0
                Alcoa Scholarship,   1972-1974
                Lassiter Scholarship, 1971-1972

PERSONAL: Married, 3 Children
                U.S. Citizen
                Excellent Health

REFERENCES: Excellent references furnished upon request.

Functional Résumé (Continued)

MARY LYNN SEIGEL
Apartment 315
Cross Creek Apartments
825 Cross Creek Road
Stanfield, Connecticut 18746

Phone: (513) 876-2948

SUMMARY: Human resources professional with 17 years
                  experience in manufacturing and consulting. Strong
                  background in executive search, employment,
                  staffing and human resources generalist areas.

MAJOR ACCOMPLISHMENTS:

Executive Search

-Senior Consultant with major international
 executive search firm (4 years).
-Successfully completed numerous assignments at
 various organizational levels (president, vice
 president, director, middle management and senior
 professional).
-Generated $180,000 revenue in third year.
-Generated $225,000 revenue in fourth year.

Employment

-Corporate Manager of Technical Employment for
 Fortune 200 company (4 years).
-Provided employment support to 4 profit centers
 (20 plants, 18,000 employees).
-Successfully staffed $1.3 billion capital
 expansion and modernization program.
-Recruited and hired 7 technical executives, 18
 technical/operations managers and 265 engineers.
-Achieved 2:1 interview to offer ratio (400%
 improvement) in 3 years.
-Achieved 1.5:1 offer to hire ratio (200%
 improvement) in 3 years.

H.R. Generalist

-Managed Human Resources and Employment Services
 Department for 1,200 employee high technology
 division.
-Managed Personnel Department for 250 employee
 non-union manufacturing plant.

Functional Résumé

WORK HISTORY:

1984 to Pres.	<u>Worthington Associates, Ltd (New York, New York)</u> Senior Consultant
1970 to 1984	<u>Carlson Electronics, Inc. (Washington, D.C.)</u>

1970 to 1984   <u>Carlson Electronics, Inc. (Washington, D.C.)</u>
Manager of Technical Employment   (1980-1984)
Manager of H.R. & Employment Servcs. (1976-1980)
Plant Personnel Manager   (1973-1976)
Personnel Assistant   (1970-1973)

EDUCATION: B.A., Bucknell University, 1970
Major: Business Administration

**PROFESSIONAL
AFFILIATIONS:**   Employment Management Association   1975-Present
    President   (1986)
    Vice President (1985)
    Secretary   (1984)
Nat. Assoc. Corp. & Prof. Recruiters 1980-1986
Nat. Assoc. Personnel Administrators 1980-1987
Human Resources Planning Society   1972-1987

PERSONAL: Married, 3 Children
U.S. Citizen
Excellent Health

REFERENCES: Excellent references furnished upon request.

Functional Résumé (Continued)

8

Employment Sources—How to Use Them

When beginning your employment search, it is important to realize that there are a number of sources that can be used to help you to find the position you are seeking. You should think creatively about the various sources that are at your disposal and how to best use them to your advantage.

Most people, when asked to list sources of jobs, will list only a relatively small number. These typically include:

Newspaper ads

Employment agencies

Executive search firms

State employment services

Actually, there are many more employment sources that can effectively be used to assist you in your job search. The purpose of this chapter is to introduce you to several of these sources and suggest ways in which they might be effectively used to help you achieve your job search objectives.

LOCAL NEWSPAPERS

The classified section of your local newspaper is perhaps the best known source of job opportunities. This does not mean, however, that it is the most productive. Knowledgeable sources estimate that only between 10 and 14 percent of all jobs filled in the United States are filled as a result of newspaper advertising. This is a fairly small percentage considering the importance attached to this source by most inexperienced job hunters. You should certainly not depend upon this as the major employment source when planning your job search campaign.

When using the local newspaper as a source in your job hunting campaign, it is important to think creatively about its use. Here are some guidelines that will help you get the most out of your news-papers:

1. Read the classified ads for specific positions that are of inter-est to you, and respond by sending a copy of your résumé along with appropriate cover letter.

2. Read the business section. Look for firms that are expanding in some way (e.g., constructing new buildings, introducing new products, installing new equipment, opening new markets, ac-quiring other companies). Also, look for signs of solid eco-nomic health (record sales & profits). Healthy, expanding firms are usually hiring and should be included among your target firms for contact. Don't ignore firms that are experienc-ing difficulty—especially if you have the skills and capability to assist them in solving their problems.

3. Carefully read announcements of internal promotions as well as new appointments from sources outside of the company.

Generally speaking, when someone is promoted there is normally need for a replacement. Likewise, in the case of external employment, the past employer will also have a spot to fill.

4. The obituary column can also be a source of job leads. If the deceased is not of retirement age, it is not uncommon for the newspaper article to list current employer and position held. In many cases, the employer will need to hire someone to fill the job vacancy.

SPECIALTY NEWSPAPERS

There are certain specialty newspapers that are geared specifically to the job hunter. These papers are normally a composite of employment ads run in major newspapers throughout the country. Two of the most popular are:

The National Ad Search

This is a weekly tabloid that is a compilation of employment want ads from seventy-two key newspapers across the United States. Over 2,000 ads are clipped, indexed and arranged into 42 executive, professional and technical categories for quick, easy reference. This weekly tabloid can be ordered by contacting National Ad Search, Inc., P.O. Box 2083, Milwaukee, WI 53101 (Phone toll-free: 1-800-992-2832).

The National Business Employment Weekly

This is a weekly tabloid published by *The Wall Street Journal* and is readily available at most newsstands and drugstores. It is a compilation of all want ad advertising run in the regional editions of *The Wall Street Journal* during the past week.

Both of these specialty newspapers can serve as excellent supplements to your local newspaper, provided, of course, you are willing to relocate to other areas of the United States. Since many of these ads are already a week or so old when they are published in these specialty papers, it is important for you to respond quickly to any ad that is of interest to you.

PROFESSIONAL ASSOCIATIONS

An important source frequently overlooked by the job seeker is professional associations. Many of these associations provide various job hunting services free of charge to their members. Such services take many forms including:

1. Computer job banks for use by both employers and individual members (The association matches employer job listings with member résumés, and forwards appropriate résumés to employer.)

2. Free job opportunity listings provided to member companies in association newsletter

3. Free *Situations Wanted* section in association's newsletter, permitting individual members to advertise their availability and summary of qualifications

4. Association sponsored job fairs where members can sign up and interview with prospective employers

5. Coordination of job hunting service programs during local, regional, or national meetings (Such coordination ranges from announcements of career opportunities at meetings, to job opportunity bulletin boards, to arranging actual interview meetings between job seeking members and prospective employers.)

All that is usually required is a little research and a few phone calls to the association's national, regional, or local headquarters. Most associations are always looking to increase their membership and welcome the opportunity to explain their services to prospective new members.

If you are unsure about how to identify associations that are related to your professional career interests, I suggest that you visit your local library and do a little research using the *Encyclopedia of*

Associations. This handy reference book lists thousands of non-profit American membership organizations of national scope, including professional societies, trade associations, labor unions, and the like. A key word index facilitates location of organizations associated with particular subjects.

TRADE/INDUSTRIAL ASSOCIATIONS

Trade or industrial associations can also prove worthwhile employment sources. As with professional associations, they frequently provide some sort of employment services to their membership. The types of services provided and methods for researching such associations are the same as with professional associations.

TRADE AND PROFESSIONAL PUBLICATIONS

Although many trade or professional associations produce their own publications, there are frequently well-read trade and professional publications that are independently published. Such publications, because of their particular focus on specific industries or professions, frequently become the targets for recruitment advertising that is specifically directed to persons having experience in these industries or occupational specialties.

Some well-spent time with the librarian in the periodical section of the library will quickly surface most of these key publications. The national officers of trade and professional associations are usually also very knowledgeable of these publications and will gladly furnish you with their names just for the asking.

EMPLOYMENT AGENCIES

There is generally a good deal of confusion among the general public concerning the difference between an employment agency and an executive search firm. Perhaps the following characteristics will help you to make the distinction:

Characteristics of Executive Search Firms

1. Hired, under contract, by employer to represent the employer's interests in identifying and recruiting candidates for a specific position

2. Legally, acts as the agent of the employer and is fully responsible to the client company for results of the search project

3. Works only on an exclusive basis (i.e., no other firm represents the employer and the employer is using no other sources to fill this position)

4. Is paid a predetermined consulting fee by the client company, regardless of the outcome of the search project (i.e., is compensated for consulting time)

5. Is reimbursed by the client company for all direct, out-of-pocket expenses incurred while conducting the search assignment

6. Always conducts a thorough, face-to-face interview with prospective candidates and prepares a complete candidate report prior to presenting candidate to client company

7. Always conducts thorough reference check and prepares complete written reference report on finalist candidates for submission to client company (Usually done prior to interview with client company)

8. Never represents job seekers in their search for employment opportunities

Characteristics of Employment Agencies

1. Generally represents the individual who is seeking employment, rather than the employer

2. May sometimes represent the employer, but there is never a binding consulting contract

3. Is never paid for consulting time—is only paid when, and if, assignment is successfully completed (i.e., position is filled)

4. Seldom has an exclusive on the assignment—must frequently compete with others to fill position

5. Is seldom, if ever, reimbursed by the employer for expenses incurred in carrying out assignment

6. Almost never conducts a face-to-face interview with candidate—uses candidate's own résumé (rather than written report) as the basis for presentation to the employer

7. Seldom, if ever, checks candidate references—no reference report submitted to employer

Employment agencies are sometimes referred to as *contingency* firms. This means that they receive no compensation unless they are successful in placing a candidate in the position. Because of this, employment agencies tend, as a group, to be considerably less objective than executive search firms. Because of the contingency nature of their operations there may be a much higher tendency to try to put a square peg in a round hole.

There are an estimated 8,000 to 10,000 employment agencies in the United States. Although there are some who do a thorough, professional job in representing employment candidates, unfortunately, there are a fair number who are simply out to make a buck, and have little concern for the interests of either the candidate or the employer. Their only concern is to quickly make a placement, collect their money, and move on to the next assignment. There are all too many of these type firms, and they have given the industry at large a very bad name. It can be difficult to know who the truly professional, reputable firms really are.

Although I would not entirely discourage use of employment agencies, I would recommend that you proceed cautiously and be sure that you are dealing with those who are ethical and professional in their dealings. In order to find out who these better firms are, I would suggest that, using your personal contacts, you secure the names of a half dozen or so Employment managers from major corporations and contact them for their recommendations on the names of some of the better agencies who specialize in your field.

Since individual consultants within the same firm can vary considerably with respect to their professionalism and effectiveness, I suggest that you also secure endorsements on the names of the better consultants in each of these recommended firms. It is best to use the names of these employment managers when contacting the recommended consultants. Tell them that they were suggested by a particular employment manager. They will normally feel flattered by this and will likely make a special effort to assist you.

When time, distance, and cost permit, you should personally visit each of the firms with whom you will be dealing. Call in advance and make an appointment with the consultant who will be representing you. During your actual visit, make sure there is a thorough understanding of your background, qualifications, and job search objectives. Failure to do this could result in improper representation of your credentials and interests, and waste considerable time for both you and the prospective employers.

If employed at the time of your job search, you will want to be particularly careful to select firms who will not expose you to unnecessary risks. In particular, you will need to be assured that your résumé will not be plastered all over the universe and that it will not be inadvertently sent to your current employer. To guard against this, you may want to control circulation of your résumé by coming to some sort of agreement with the agency counselor concerning the specific circumstances under which your résumé would be presented to a particular employer. Additionally, so there are no mistakes, you may also want to furnish this counselor with the names of all divisions, subsidiaries, and affiliate companies that are part of, or associated with, your current employer.

As an additional word of caution, when using employment agencies, many of these firms are members of large associations that share résumés and job listings with other associations members. Some of the larger of these associations have several thousand member firms. If currently employed, mass circulation of your résumé to association membership, with subsequent mailing by these member firms as part of a mass promotional mailing, may not exactly be in your best interests. I would recommend, where this is the case, that you advise the employment agency that your résumé is not to be mailed to any association members without your specific approval and, under no circumstances, is it to be made available to the general association membership.

In addition to the obvious risk of being found out by your current employer, there is also the danger that a given employer will receive several copies of your résumé from different sources. This mass broadcasting suggests to potential employers that your job campaign lacks focus and control. It also suggests that you are not using proper discretion and care in conducting your campaign if, as your résumé suggests, you are currently employed. This may also suggest that perhaps you no longer have need to be concerned about being found out by your current employer (e.g., have already been terminated). Thus, as you can see, it is important to control distribution of your résumé.

As a final caution, since employment agency fees are not always paid by the employer, it is important, when accepting the opportunity for an interview with one of the agency's client companies, to determine whether this company is willing to pay the agency fee if you are subsequently hired by that firm. These fees are substantial and should not be taken lightly. The norm is one percent for every $1,000 of the first year's annual compensation (maximum fee of 30 percent). Thus, a position paying $40,000 could have an agency fee of $12,000; a $50,000 job a fee of $15,000; an $80,000 job a fee of $24,000, etc. Although most companies will pay the agency fee for hiring professional or managerial talent, this is not always the case. Considering the size of these fees, this is not an item to be left to chance.

If you have difficulty in identifying a half dozen or so employment managers from whom you can secure recommendations on the more reputable employment agencies, a suitable alternative might be to secure references from the agency itself. Ask the agency representative, with whom you would be working, for the names of four or five employment managers with whom they have worked on a regular basis. Tell him or her that you would like to talk with these references before establishing a working relationship. By all means, check these references carefully before proceeding to work with the firm. Here are some questions you could use to check these references:

1. How long have you dealt with the ABC Agency?

2. What has been the nature of this association?

3. How satisfied have you been with their thoroughness and professionalism?

4. What criticisms, if any, might you have concerning their performance?

5. Have you had much occasion to work with Consultant X?

6. What has been the nature of that working relationship?

7. What observations can you make about Consultant X's thoroughness and professionalism?

8. From your observations, what are his/her strengths?

9. What are his or her shortcomings, if any?

10. If you were considering a job change, would you use his or her services? Why? Why not?

Answers to these questions should put you in a position to know whether this is the type of firm with which you should be working. It is important to the success of your campaign that you be represented by persons who will be thorough, professional, and have your career interests at heart. You certainly want to avoid money-hungry hucksters who will try to sell your soul to the first bidder for a quick buck, so don't short-cut this reference checking procedure. Know that the persons who will be representing you can be trusted and will accurately represent both your qualifications and interests to prospective employers.

If you are certain about how to identify employment agencies with specialization in your industry or profession, there are a few things that you can do to flush this out. Some of the better sources for securing this information are the various trade or professional journals relating to your areas of interest. You will find that many of the better agencies, having specialization in these areas, will advertise in these highly-targeted publications. The officers of trade and professional associations will usually know who the key players are. They can also suggest the journals, relating to their fields, that are likely to contain recruitment ads of these specialty agencies. So, with a few well-placed phone calls, you will be able to quickly identify the firms with whom you should definitely be in contact.

It is important, however, that you not overestimate the importance of employment agencies as an employment source. Various studies conclude that only between nine and twelve percent of all jobs filled in the United States are filled by employment agencies. If you are a serious job hunter, it is important that you not rely solely on the use of employment agencies, but rather make use of a wide array of employment sources when conducting your job search campaign.

EXECUTIVE SEARCH FIRMS

Although you should not overlook the use of executive search firms when conducting your job search, you should not overestimate potential results. In fact, although these firms are usually highly professional, they are less likely to be able to help you than the employment agencies. There are several different reasons for this.

First, because of the highly-focused nature of their business, each consultant may only be conducting three to five executive search assignments simultaneously (unlike the employment agency where the number is likely to be ten to twenty positions). When your résumé hits the door, the odds are great that the search firm will not currently be working on an assignment that is related to your qualifications and interests. Since, by the nature of their business, they represent the employer rather than the job seeker, you can be reasonably assured that, unless they just coincidentally have an assignment that matches your background, you will not be hearing from them. The most you can expect is that you will receive a brief letter or postcard acknowledging receipt of your résumé and notifying you that they are not currently working on an assignment conducive to your interests.

Although the odds are against you, there may still be good reasons for sending your résumé to executive search firms. This is particularly true if you are employed in a management capacity and have 1987 earnings of $50,000 or higher. Currently, most executive search firms have a salary cutoff of $50,000 and will not conduct search assignments for client companies where the compensation level of the position is below the $50,000 level. Thus, if you are earning considerably below this level, don't waste your time. By contrast, if you are employed in a management or executive position and are earning over $50,000 (1987 basis), it is recommended that you make a broadcast mailing of your résumé to these firms. If you have good credentials, you can be assured that your résumé will be filed for reference in the event a future search assignment is undertaken by the firm that is a suitable match for your qualifications and interests.

Unlike the employment agency, you do not have to be concerned that the search firm will mail your résumé all over the place. To the contrary, they will not present a candidate's credentials to a client company without first conducting an indepth, face-to-face interview, followed by a thorough check of references. You are assured of your confidentiality and there is almost no risk whatsoever in forwarding your credentials to these firms. Additionally, since the consulting fees of the executive search firm are always paid by the client company whom they serve, there is absolutely no cost to you, should this contact result in your employment by the client organization.

There is one word of caution when it comes to dealing with executive search firms: *Beware of the impostors!* Unfortunately, it has become popular for employment agencies to refer to themselves as executive search firms, when in fact they are not. This practice has served to seriously blur the distinction between the two in the mind of the public. The acid test has to do with the method by which these firms are compensated for their services.

The true executive search consulting firm works only on a fully retained basis. As consultants, they are compensated for their consulting time, regardless of the outcome of the search assignments. Normally their fees range between 30 and 35 percent of the estimated first year's annual compensation of a successful candidate. These fees are usually paid by the client company in three equal installments over the first three months of the search assignment. If cancellation of the assignment occurs within these first three months, the total fee is prorated accordingly and the search firm is compensated for actual time spent on the search.

Employment agencies, on the other hand, fall into two categories based upon how they are compensated—contingency firms and retained contingency. As the term suggests, agencies who work on a contingency basis are only entitled to a fee (from either the candidate or the company) when they have successfully placed a candidate in the job. Such firms have not been retained by the client organization, and the client organization, therefore, has no legal obligation whatsoever to pay the agent's fee. In such case, the job seeker is very much at risk, and may end up with a legal obligation to pay the agency fee if successfully placed with an employer.

The retained contingency firms, although still technically an employment agency, usually have a much stronger working relationship with the client company. These firms usually require the client firm, who has retained their services, to pay a portion (usually one-third) of their fee at the onset of the assignment, with the balance (usually two-thirds) to be paid contingent upon successful placement of a candidate in the position. Here again, as with the contingency agency, they are not truly consultants and are thus compensated on the basis of results rather than their consulting time.

Hopefully this discussion has served to clarify the difference between the employment agency and the executive search firm. It should also be clear that the executive search firms generally stand at the top of their profession, are very knowledgeable and professional, and are compensated as professional consultants for their consulting time.

What does all of this have to do with your job search? Simply this: If you want to avoid the risk of having your résumé plastered like wallpaper all over the place, you will want to avoid indiscriminately mailing it out to employment agencies. You must therefore know how to tell the difference between the agency and the search firm (to whom you will clearly want to mail your résumé). Additionally, it is important to make this distinction so that you are not suddenly surprised with the possible presentation of a rather sizeable bill for the agent's services.

The trick is to secure a listing of the fully retained executive search firms to be included in your mail campaign. Fortunately, most of these firms belong to one of two organizations. The first is the AESC (Association of Executive Search Consultants), headquartered in Greenwich, Connecticut. The second, a newer organization, is the NACPR (National Association of Corporate and Professional Recruiters), headquartered in Stamford, Connecticut. The NACPR has offices throughout the United States, and can be located by calling information in some of the larger cities (New York, Philadelphia, Boston, etc.). You should contact both of these associations to see how you might secure a copy of their membership directory.

When mailing your résumé to executive search firms, be sure to mail copies to all offices of each firm, not just the firm's corporate offices. Don't assume because they are the firm's corporate offices that your résumé will automatically be available to other regional offices. This may not be the case and you could easily eliminate consideration of your employment candidacy for a highly desirable position being handled by one of the firm's branch offices.

Likewise, if you are unwilling to relocate or otherwise have geographical restrictions, don't simply mail your résumé to the regional office closest to your desired geographical area. In most cases, consultants of executive search firms are not limited to working in a certain geographical region. Instead, they tend to be functional or industry specialists, and work with clients on a national, if not international, basis. Thus, a consultant working out of the San Francisco office is likely to have clients located in Philadelphia, New York, or Atlanta, and although unlikely, may not have a single client in the San Francisco area. To further make my point on geography, my firm, Wellington Management Group, a Philadelphia-based executive search consulting firm, has over 85 percent of its client base located outside of the Philadelphia area. Current clients include firms who are located in Atlanta, Dallas, Chicago, New York and the west coast. So, here again, my advice is to mail your résumé to all offices of these firms, not just those offices that are closest to your area of geographical preference.

Although many career counselors and outplacement firms may advise you differently, I do not recommend making *cold calls* to the offices of executive search consulting firms. You would do better with a dart board at a hundred yards. Most consultants simply refuse to take unsolicited calls from job seekers. The experienced ones have long ago come to realize that taking such calls is a poor use of their time. Additionally, your time can be more constructively utilized by focusing on other sources that are likely to prove productive in achieving your job search objectives. Send your résumé. Don't call. You will hear soon enough if the consultant has a search assignment for which you are a possible candidate. Calling to discuss your background, when it is extremely unlikely that the consultant is currently working on an appropriate search assignment, is hardly an effective use of valuable time. So, don't call. Invest your time and energy elsewhere.

ALUMNI ASSOCIATIONS

Many colleges and universities offer employment or placement services to their alumni. In the case of larger schools, there is often an alumni placement office set up for this very purpose. Some of these are quite active and maintain close ties with major employers who frequently recruit on their campus for recent college graduates.

In most cases the alumni placement office serves as clearing house for résumés submitted by its alumni. Employers list job openings with the alumni placement office, whose staff then compares the requirements of these positions with résumés of alumni on file, forwarding the résumés of qualified persons to the listing employer. Placement can sometimes result.

This source, although not normally very productive, seems to work best where the school has strong recruiting relationships with the employer, and the firm has had a long history of recruiting graduates from a particular curriculum. For instance, if the school has long had an excellent reputation for its curriculum in Packaging Engineering, and there are a number of companies who recruit there for that purpose, there is a high likelihood that when the same companies are in need of an experienced packaging engineer, they will think of this school as a potential source and contact the alumni placement office.

With the exception of those schools who enjoy an excellent reputation for a given educational discipline, alumni placement offices are not usually very productive job sources, and should not be thought of as a major employment source when planning your job search campaign. They can occasionally be helpful, so should not be ignored altogether.

A quick phone call to your alma mater is all that it takes to determine if it provides job placement assistance to its alumni. Inquire about the necessary procedures on how to get your résumé into their system and, by all means, send them a copy of your employment résumé at your earliest convenience. What do you have to lose? And, best of all, it costs no more than the cost of postage. This is hardly an avenue you should pass up.

JOB FAIRS AND RECRUITING CONFERENCES

The job fair or recruiting conference has long been a tool used by companies to recruit hard-to-find talent. Most often, it has been used by the aerospace, defense electronics, and computer industries to recruit hard-to-find technical talent (engineers, scientists, computer programmers, etc.). They have also been used, however, as a method for the recruitment of persons with generic skills that can be applied across companies and industries (accounting, sales, etc.). For the most part, such conferences are used by participating companies as a way to fill junior level organization openings (i.e., those requiring one to five years of experience).

Job fairs and recruiting conferences have been organized by both employers (especially when they have a number of similar openings) and individual entrepreneurs, who are motivated by profit. In most cases there is no fee charged to the candidate participants. Instead, employers who are participating are required to pay a base registration for participation in the conference, plus a fee for each successful hiring that results from conference interviews. In some cases, however, the candidate applicant may also be charged a registration fee, as well. It's best to determine what your financial obligations will be in advance of your participation. In this way, there are no surprises later on.

One of the key attractions of a job fair or recruiting conference is that it potentially provides you with the opportunity to interview with more than one employer in the span of a one- or two-day period. It is advisable to find out what the interview ground rules are in advance of your attendance, so that you are not disappointed.

In some conferences, employers are permitted closed schedules. This means they have the opportunity to prescreen the résumés of attendees in advance (or at the beginning) of the conference, designating to the conference managers which of the candidates they wish to interview. In such cases they are under no obligation to interview any other conference participants. Thus, if it is a closed schedule conference, you may or may not have the opportunity to interview with those employers in whom you have the most interest.

On the other hand, an open schedule conference means that you have the opportunity to sign up with any of the conference attendees, and, provided there is space on their interview schedule, they are obligated to grant you an employment interview. An open schedule may be more to your advantage; however, this would depend upon the employers who are scheduled to be in attendance.

Prior to investing in registration fees and the expenses of travel and lodging, it would pay to do some advance research. Call the group responsible for organization and management of the conference and ask the following questions:

1. What are the fees for registration?

2. What fees, if any, will be payable by you, should you be hired by one of the employers attending the conference?

3. How many employers will be attending the conference?

4. Which, if any, are firms from your job search target group?

5. What are the positions for which these firms will be recruiting?

6. Are the interview sign-up schedules closed or open?

7. If closed schedules, when and how do you determine which employers have expressed an interest in you?

8. How many candidates will be in attendance at the conference?

Generally speaking, the better conferences are those where all costs are borne by the employers who are in attendance. A willingness to pay all conference and resultant placement fees by the employer is usually a good sign that the employers feel that such conferences are a valuable source of employment candidates. Such employer willingness to pay these fees is also usually a sign that the firms who will be in attendance are worthwhile, rather than fly-by-night organizations.

Be somewhat wary of those conferences where the fees are to be borne by the candidate attendees. Such arrangements usually suggest that the conference sponsors are more interested in collecting fees from attendees than doing something meaningful that will result in solid employment opportunities. If in doubt, ask for the names, and contact information from four or five attendees who attended the last conference sponsored by this group. Make sure you are investing your time and money wisely.

If you are interested in finding out more about career conferences or job fairs that focus on your industry or professional specialty, a good source can be the national office of your trade or professional association. They are usually aware of who the sponsoring organizations are and how to contact them. Also, sponsoring organizations often advertise upcoming job fairs and career conferences in the trade journals and newsletters related to the industry or professional specialty they are targeting. These conferences are also frequently advertised in major metropolitan newspapers in the want ad section.

COMPUTER JOB BANKS

The origin of computer job banks dates back at least 15 years. The underlying concept behind these banks is the ability to use the computer to match applicant qualification to a preloaded list of jobs specifications, thus being able to identify qualified candidates for these positions.

Computer job banks, for the most part, have been the brainchild of entrepreneurial individuals who saw this as a concept for making lots of money. The idea is to market this system both ways—to the job seeker as well as the employer. Typically the job seeker is charged a registration fee (ranging from $25 to several hundred dollars) for the privilege of inputting basic data extracted from a résumé into the computer data base. On the other side of the ledger, companies are then charged a fee to access this data base to search out persons having certain qualifications. For this, they may pay a one-time access fee or a general access fee that entitles them to access the data base for a defined period (usually a year).

Every time I think of these candidate search data bases, I am reminded of the time a vendor of such a system, who shall remain nameless, came to my office at Scott Paper Company to demonstrate his wares. (At the time, I worked in the Corporate Employment Department as Manager of Technical Employment.) At the time of this vendor's visit, we were in the process of recruiting a large number of engineers to staff a major $1.3 billion capital expansion project.

The vendor represented a very large, multibillion dollar company, who decided that this would be an effective way to market a voluminous data base of engineering talent that they had accumulated as a result of their own recruiting efforts. The vendor had with him a desktop computer and modum which could be used to access the data base in the firm's main computer, back at corporate headquarters. Although time has blurred my memory a bit (this was 1975), I believe that the data base contained somewhere in excess of 25,000 engineers.

After some initial difficulty in hooking up the computer and accessing the main data base, my guest then proceeded to conduct a live test of how this data base was supposed to work. Taking one of the positions for which I was recruiting (which, by the way, required a fairly generic profile), I provided the vendor with about 14 or 15 selection factors, each of which was diligently inputted into the system. The vendor then gave the computer the necessary command to commence search of the data base for our candidate. After a few seconds of search, a message appeared on the screen to the effect that no such candidate existed within the data base. We then repeated the search four or five times, each time using fewer and fewer of the original 14 or 15 selection criteria.

Finally, after several false starts, we were able to generate a printout of available candidates, each with a brief biographical summary of qualifications. By now, however, the list of selection criteria used on the final search was so watered down, compared to the original selection criteria, that the list of candidates generated was almost meaningless. Additionally, the data provided on each supposedly qualified candidate was so general that it was impossible to tell for sure whether the candidates were truly viable for the position we were trying to fill. We then repeated the experiment using several other positions and specifications with similar results. In each case, there were few, if any, candidates identified. Where identified, there was insufficient information available about the candidate upon which to base a decision. The next step would have been to request a hard copy of each candidate's résumé, which would have been sent to us by mail. This was hardly a timesaving, efficient system. Needless to say, we elected not to subscribe to this network.

This story serves to illustrate a point. Although computers, I'm sure, have advanced to the point of having the capability to handle such a system, to the best of my knowledge no one has developed a sufficiently good system to make this application a truly viable concept. Typically, the problems with such data bases are:

1. Insufficient number of candidate entries to make the system attractive to employer users.

2. Insufficient number of job entries to make the system attractive to candidate users.

3. The time and cost necessary to keep candidate and job listings current is usually prohibitive, thus resulting in a data base that is chock-full of obsolete data.

4. The number of candidate or job selection criteria variables is enormous, making it difficult to input sufficient information to allow for meaningful identification and selection. (Results are poor matching or insufficient data upon which to make a good decision.)

Although computers would now appear to have the capacity to handle the necessary information to create an effective candidate/ job search system, the development of good software for making such systems viable appears to be lagging considerably behind. I suppose with the computer capacity being there, however, it's just a matter of time before some creative and hard-working software designer will develop the software to make this a practical and worthwhile concept. In the meantime, be cautious about paying any sizeable fees for either accessing a job bank or inputting your credentials into a candidate search system.

If tempted to make use of a computerized job bank, before paying your access fee I would suggest that you get answers to the following basic questions:

1. How many total employers are represented in the job bank?

2. How many of these employers are from your target industries?

3. How current is the data base?

4. What is the system for maintaining the data base?

5. What is the basis for selecting jobs for entry (i.e., what is the source of jobs; what are the criteria for entry)?

6. How frequently are new listings inputted?

7. What is the basis for purging listings from the data base?

8. How often is data purged?

9. What are the variables which can be used for screening the data base? What are the limitations?

10. What are the access fees?

11. What is the frequency and limitations on access?

12. Will the vendor provide a demonstration (using unrelated position, of course)?

A similar set of questions needs to be asked if the data base is one that lists candidates, as opposed to jobs. The presumption here is that the data base will be used by employers to identify candidates for current openings within their organization. These questions are:

1. How many total employers are currently subscribers to the data base?

2. How many of these are from target industries?

3. How many job seekers are contained in the data base?

4. What is the breakout of functional disciplines represented by these candidates?

5. Does the data base focus on industry, or functional specialties, or is it a general data base?

6. What has been the frequency of employer inquiries of the data base? In the last year? In the last month?

7. How current is the data base?

8. How often is it purged?

9. What determines when a candidate's file is purged?

10. What are the fees for inputting your data?

11. Exactly what information will be inputted from your résumé? What is excluded?

12. How long will your information remain on file in the data base?

13. What safeguards exist that would prevent disclosure of your information to your current employer, should your employer or any of its affiliates have access to the data base?

If currently employed, one major danger of using this kind of candidate data base as part of your job hunting campaign is the danger that your employer may discover that you are on the job market. It is particularly important, therefore, that there be safeguards in effect that would prevent release of your computer file to either your current employer or to one of its affiliate companies. Additionally, if access to the data base is not controlled and, for example, employment agencies are allowed access, your risks are substantially increased. It is, therefore, your responsibility to determine the types of controls that are exercised by the data base manager to prevent this unnecessary risk and potentially embarrassing exposure.

To date, computer job banks have not proven a highly effective job hunting source. There are simply too many limitations and risks associated with them to make them very useful. Although you might want to use them to supplement other more viable sources, don't let them play a major role in your job hunting campaign. Perhaps, as software development and security controls become more sophisticated, these computer systems may begin to take on an increasingly more fruitful role in the job search campaign. At this stage, however, they continue to be relatively ineffective and risky when compared to many other job sources.

CAREER CONSULTANTS

The field of career and job search consulting is exploding. The recent downsizing of the middle management segment of American industry, coupled with sweetened early retirement and separation programs, has caused a flood of middle management and seasoned professionals on the job market. Most of these are people needing job hunting assistance of some type, ranging all the way from résumé preparation assistance to the planning of full-fledged job search marketing programs with all the bells and whistles. Many of these managers and professionals have not been on the job markets for 15 to 20 years and, for the most part, are at a total loss on how to organize and plan an effective job hunting campaign.

Along with this demand for employment assistance, has come the birth and explosion of an entirely new industry—the outplacement consulting practice. Only a decade ago, the idea of companies paying sizeable fees to consultants for providing job hunting training and assistance to terminated employees, was almost unheard of. At that time, assistance, if provided at all, was usually limited to some basic counseling on résumé preparation, and rudimentary job hunting techniques provided by the employer's personnel or employment manager. For older, seasoned employees who have been out of the job market for several years, such basic counseling proved woefully inadequate with the consequence that many of these employees were months in making a successful employment transition (if ever).

In recent years with the current emphasis on employee headcount reduction as an important method of cost reduction and achievement of competitive advantage, the concept of company-paid outplacement job hunting assistance has come of age. Motivated by a combination of social responsibility and the threat of expensive litigation from terminated employees, many companies now employ professional outplacement consultants to run full-fledged job search training programs for their terminated employees. There are company-sponsored outplacement centers that house and nurture these employees during the sometimes lengthy and arduous job hunting process. For this, they can pay these consultants rather sizeable fees ranging from a couple of hundred dollars for simple résumé preparation assistance, to several thousand dollars for a highly-individualized job search planning and support program. Fees charged for more elaborate programs can run as high as 10 to 15 percent of the terminated employee's annual salary, plus reimbursement of the consultant's out-of-pocket expenses. Thus the outplacement fee for a $100,000 executive could run as high as $10,000 to $15,000.

Although many of these professional outplacement consulting firms provide their services only to employers, some will undertake individual counseling, as well. This can be a fairly expensive proposition, so you will want to be sure of what you are getting for your money. For the most part, professional, reputable firms offer a fairly comprehensive service including:

1. Some minor psychological counseling to assist you in making the transition from being employed to being unemployed, and to put you into a positive frame of mind as you begin the job hunting process

2. Some career and job counseling aimed at helping you to define realistic, obtainable job hunting objectives

3. Assistance in preparing a professional, effective résumé

4. Training in the use of numerous job hunting and job reference sources

5. Training in the use of various job hunting techniques (especially emphasizing the networking process)

6. Training in effective interviewing techniques (along with practice interviews followed by professional critique)

7. Use of a professional job search center including all support services (library, phones, typing & secretarial support)

8. Continued counseling and support throughout the job search process, as needed

In addition to these professional outplacement firms, which generally provide their services to corporations, there have been a whole host of employment and career counseling firms that have sprung up to meet the needs of the individual job seeker. The more reputable ones provide training and services substantially similar to those provided by the outplacement consultant. Unfortunately, along with these ethical and reputable firms, numerous less reputable firms have emerged to fill the void. These purveyors of snake oil and quick-fix bromides have one thing in common: They are out to dazzle you with their fancy footwork and lighten your wallet, without providing you with any meaningful job hunting assistance.

I have been involved with the job hunting process, in one way or another, for over 20 years, and believe me when I say, "There are no shortcuts to the job search process." Successful job hunting requires three things: patience, persistence, and plenty of hard work. There are no quick, easy fixes that will allow you to short-cut the process and find meaningful employment in a short time frame. As testimony to this, consider the fact that most knowledgeable outplacement firms, even with their sophisticated training techniques, estimate that, on average, it takes about one month of job search time for every $10,000 of annual earnings to find a meaningful job. Thus, an executive earning $100,000 can expect to look for ten months; a $60,000 executive, six months; a $40,000 professional, four months, etc. The logic behind this says, the higher the job level, the fewer are the jobs at this level, and the longer it takes to find such a position. Conversely, the lower the job level, the more plentiful are the jobs and the shorter is the job search.

Beware of those consultants who claim they can help you find a job quickly, or who claim they have some magical method for helping you to find that job that you've always dreamed of. Also, beware of the gimmicks—things like exclusive lists of key openings, elaborate computer matching services, special inside contacts who will help get interviews, special computer mailing lists of key contacts, etc. Generally, the more ludicrous the claim, the higher the probability that you'll be dealing with a crook who is a sure expert in one area only—parting you from your hard-earned money.

Don't fall for gimmickry. Plain and simply, successful job hunting requires nothing less than good old persistence and hard work. So, keep your money in your pocket and follow the advice in this book.

If you do feel compelled to use the services of a professional job search consultant, take the time to check the firm out. Make sure

that the firm is completely aboveboard and that your money is
going to be well-spent. To be sure that you are dealing with a
reputable firm, before spending any money, get answers to the
following questions:

1. How long has the firm been in business?

2. How many persons have they counseled over the years?

3. What has been their success rate? How many of their clients
   have found meaningful work? What has been the average
   length of time needed to find work?

4. What are the total fees?

5. What do you get for your investment (i.e., the components of
   their program)?

6. What are the qualifications of your counselor(s)?

7. What direct employment experience has this counselor(s)
   had (e.g., search firm, employment manager, employment
   agency), if any?

8. What guarantees, if any, do they provide?

If you get relatively good answers to these questions and feel that
you might wish to go ahead with their service, take one additional
step—ask for references. Request the names and contact information on at least four or five persons who have recently gone through
their program. If you are told that the names of their clients are
confidential and they can, therefore, not honor your request, tell
them to contact these clients and get permission to release this information to you. If they balk at this request, I have one final piece of
advice: Hang on to your wallet and get out of there as fast as you can!

On the other hand, if the consultant provides you with the references that you have requested, make sure to check them thoroughly before proceeding. Here are some suggested questions that
might be used in doing this:

1. If you don't mind sharing this information with me, what did you pay for the services of the ABC Company?

2. What, specifically, did you get for your money?

3. Overall, how would you rate their program?

4. In what areas did the program meet or exceed your expectations?

5. In what areas did the program fall short of your expectations?

6. In what ways could the program have been made more meaningful?

7. If you knew what you now know about this program, would you take it again? Why?

8. Was it a good value for the money, or is it overpriced?

As a final step, having completed this reference check, contact the local Better Business Bureau to find out whether there have been any recent complaints filed against the company in question. If so, how many and what have been the nature of these complaints? Additionally, you might contact some of the personnel and employment managers working for area companies to find out what they can tell you about the company.

If a thorough reference check turns up little or no negative information, chances are you are safe to proceed, and that you will be getting a quality service for your money. In general, however, you can probably do just as much for yourself by reading a couple of good books on the subject of job hunting. Most of what these firms offer to do in the form of consulting services can be done by you, and you can save a lot of money in the process.

BUSINESS CONSULTING FIRMS

Firms engaged in providing consulting services to companies (i.e., strategic planning, marketing, accounting, financial, and human resource consulting) are many times aware of potential job openings long before these openings hit the street. Such firms can therefore prove to be a noteworthy source for identifying new job opportunities.

Unfortunately, unless you have a close personal contact with the consulting firm, these advance leads may be extremely difficult to get. Since these firms are privy to a great deal of confidential information regarding such things as new products, new market strategy, acquisitions, joint ventures, capital expansions, etc., they are often aware of the possibility of opportunities. In many cases, because of this confidentiality, however, they are not at liberty to share this information with you. There is nothing to stop them from recommending you or passing your résumé along to the right party, however.

As part of your employment strategy, therefore, it would probably be a good idea to cultivate some friendships with principals or consultants employed by these types of consulting firms.

BANKS AND ATTORNEYS

As with consulting firms, banks and attorneys are often aware of organizational changes that could result in staffing needs within client organizations. With this in mind, it is probably a good idea, when possible, to cultivate some relationships in these type firms, as well. These relationships could lead to a personal recommendation or job lead referral.

STATE EMPLOYMENT SERVICE

The State Employment Service, known within some states as the Bureau of Employment Security, has, as its main purpose, the objective of helping unemployed workers to find employment. The law in many states requires employers to list all job openings with the State Employment Service so these positions can be listed on a master list for use by the state's employment counselors. Sometimes, these lists are computerized, and it is possible to use the computer to search the list for job openings that may be appropriate to your background and interests.

Although in many states the law provides for mandatory listing of job openings, my impression is that this is not often well-policed and, as a result, many openings never appear on the list. Nonetheless, as part of your job search campaign, it is probably a good idea to visit the State Employment Service to find out what resources are available to help you in your job search. Although, historically, the states have been far more successful in finding jobs for blue collar workers, there is always the possibility that some real assistance could be forthcoming. In any event, access to the computerized job bank may be just the thing that makes this a worthwhile trip.

This, like the alumni placement office, is another one of those free services that should not be overlooked as you plan and execute your job search strategy. As the saying goes, *Check your telephone directory for the office nearest you.*

9

The Direct Mail Campaign

Use of the direct mail campaign is a fairly common job hunting technique that has been around for quite a number of years. If carefully designed and executed, it can be a productive source of interviews and employment opportunities. The key words here are *designed* and *executed*. If little time and effort are put into the design and execution of this job search method, it can be a complete waste of time.

Who should use a direct mail campaign? When should it be used? How is an effective campaign planned and executed? What are the steps needed to ensure success? This chapter will provide answers to these questions as well as a step-by-step process for designing and executing an effective campaign. If carefully followed, the advice provided here should enable you to design your own direct mail campaign and to effectively target it to help you in achieving your job search objective.

No job hunting method or technique can guarantee good results. The direct mail campaign is no exception to this rule and, at most, will provide only a partial answer to your job hunting needs. It makes sense, therefore, to view this as only one component of your total job hunting program. It should, by no means, represent your sole method for finding employment.

WHEN TO USE THE DIRECT MAIL CAMPAIGN

The direct mail campaign is generally used by those who are currently employed, and cannot commit a significant amount of time to the job search process. One of the key advantages of this technique is that it is a method that can be planned and executed during evenings and weekends, which does not interfere with one's work schedule. It is commonly used as a substitute for the networking process (described in the next chapter) by those who simply cannot expend the necessary time to carry out a full-blown networking process.

It is the opinion of this author, and one that is shared by most employment and outplacement professionals, that networking is, by far, a much more effective job search technique than is the mail campaign. Unfortunately, however, networking is very time consuming, and does not lend itself well to those who are currently employed. From a practical standpoint, employed persons don't normally have the necessary freedom to make the numerous telephone calls and personal contacts that are essential to making the networking process a success. The direct mail campaign can play a much larger role in the employed individual's job hunting campaign.

This does not mean that employed persons should ignore the networking process. To the contrary, they should clearly use it as a job hunting method. Time constraints will dictate, however, that networking will play a substantially reduced role in the total search process of those who are employed. Conversely, by virtue of these same constraints, the mail campaign will assume a much larger role.

On the other hand, the direct mail campaign should certainly not be ignored as a job hunting method by those currently unemployed. It is an effective method that can be used to supplement the networking process. Since networking has historically proven itself to be a far more productive method than the direct mail campaign, however, those who are unemployed should place less emphasis on the mail campaign and commit the bulk of their time to the networking technique. In such cases, the direct mail campaign should be used only as a means of contacting those target firms where, after considerable effort, it was not possible to use personal contacts to network. It should also be used as a supplemental technique to contact secondary target companies, where, due to the size of the primary target group, personal contact with these secondary firms is not a practical consideration.

Whether employed or unemployed, the direct mail campaign should be included in all job hunting campaigns. In both cases, the method for planning and executing an effective mail campaign is identical.

KEY STEPS

The key steps of an effective mail campaign are fairly straight forward. They are:

1. Design of cover letter
2. Research of target industry (or geography)
3. Identification of target executive
4. Actual mailing

We will use this chapter to systematically explore each of these components and to make suggestions which should help to increase the effectiveness of this employment search technique. By following each of these steps, in the sequence provided, you should be able to plan and execute an effective direct mail campaign.

Designing the Cover Letter

Design of an effective cover letter for a broadcast campaign need not be a particularly difficult task. Essentially, the letter is comprised of the following elements:

1. Return address

2. Date

3. Employer's name and address

4. Salutation

5. Introductory paragraph

6. Statement of purpose

7. Brief summary of qualifications

8. Request for response

9. Closing and signature

Some sample broadcast cover letters are shown on the next few pages. Study them carefully and use them as models for designing your own cover letter for use with your direct mail campaign.

Research Methodology

Once you have designed an effective broadcast cover letter for use in your direct mail campaign, your next step is to research your primary target industry to develop a list of target companies for

825 Stoney Hill Road
Portland, OR 17635
January 18, 1988

Ms. Mary Ann McQuail
President
Wharton Manufacturing Company
1771 Well Station Road
Dallas, Texas 98725

Dear Ms. McQuail:

As President and Chief Executive Officer of a leading firm
in the field of hardware manufacturing, I am sure that you
are aware of the importance and value of a top flight Chief
Financial Officer on your staff. If you are in need of such
an individual, you may wish to give serious consideration to
my credentials.

With over 15 years of progressively senior accounting and
financial management positions in the hardware manufacturing
industry, I have logged some notable achievements in such
important areas as cash flow improvement, profit
enhancement, and improved management reporting, through
application of modern computer software packages. In my
current assignment as Chief Financial Officer for a $40
million manufacturer of industrial fasteners, for example, I
initiated important programs that have earned nearly $2
million savings through modern cost tracking and targeting
methods.

Although I have found my current position quite satisfying
from the professional standpoint, Dutrar Company is family
owned. For this reason, it would appear that future
advancement opportunities may not be available. I have thus
decided to search for a new professional position that
offers better future growth possibilities.

My compensation requirements are in the $90,000 range plus
comprehensive benefits package.

I would welcome the opportunity to explore appropriate
opportunities with you firm, and would hope to hear from you
in the near future.

Thank you for your consideration.

                              Sincerely,

                              Richard B. Smith

        Broadcast Cover Letter

816 Clayton Avenue
Allentown, Pa 17365
December 17, 1978

Mr. Martin Clansberry
Director of Manufacturing
Carlston Tube Manufacturing, Inc.
127 First Street
Reading, CA 28736

Dear Mr. Clansberry:

A decision was recently made to close the Allentown plant of
Falstrom Tube Company, where I have been employed as
Operations Manager for the last five years. I am thus
seeking a responsible position in manufacturing management
with a company engaged in the manufacture of similar
products, where my skills and extensive experience can be
fully utilized.

My background includes over 20 years of experience in copper
tubing manufacturing. This includes nearly 15 years in a
management capacity. I have had an excellent record of
consistently high level performance and meaningful
contribution. In the last five years, for example, I have
increased production output by nearly 18% while
simultaneously reducing costs by 23%. I was cited for
outstanding performance in 1986, and awarded the President's
Award along with a sizeable bonus.

I hold an M.S. in Metallurgical Engineering and am
up-to-date on modern manufacturing methodology. I am
thoroughly trained and experienced in such concepts as
total quality, statistical process control, and just in time
management. I have also had experience working with new
organization effectiveness and socio-technical management
concepts.

I have no geographical preferences or restrictions. Salary
requirements are in the mid $70,000 range and are
negotiable, as appropriate, with the specific opportunity.

I look forward to hearing from you.

Sincerely,

Ralph F. Braun

Broadcast Cover Letter

158

142 East 42nd Street
Apartment 125
New York, New York 19873
October 24, 1987

Mr. Stephen Johnson
Vice President R & D
Dexter Pharmaceutical Company
875 Braxton Hollow Road
Springfield, MA 17635

Dear Mr. Johnson:

Because of your outstanding reputation as a leader in the field of biogenetic research, I am interested in exploring the possibility of employment as a senior scientist in your Research & Development function.

In addition to my technical qualifications as set forth in the enclosed resume, I feel that it is important for you to know that I have a reputation for creative solutions to the unusually difficult technical problems. I also possess the ability to translate market need into practical laboratory solutions. As a result, I enjoy an excellent reputation with marketing management for developing products uniquely suited to defined market requirements. This has greatly facilitated market planning and enabled the company to consistently achieve market objectives.

While I have enjoyed my employment with Diamond Chemical Company, the decision was recently made to sell the biotechnology division, the division with which I am employed. This impending sale, coupled with resultant future uncertainty, has prompted me to seek employment elsewhere.

My current compensation is in the low $70,000 range. I will require a comparable offer along with appropriate assistance with relocation costs.

Thank you for your consideration. I look forward to hearing from you shortly.

Sincerely,

Keith Larson

Broadcast Cover Letter

159

your mailing list. There are several good sources that can be used for this purpose. These are:

1. *Thomas' Register*

   Thomas Publishing Company, 461 Eighth Avenue, New York, New York 10001.

   Lists 100,000 manufacturers by product and location.

2. *Moody's Industrial Manual, Volume One*

   Moody's Investment Service, 99 Church Street, New York, New York 10007.

   Provides a classification of thousands of companies by industries and products.

3. *Directory of Directories*

   Gale Research Company, Book Tower, Detroit, Michigan 48226.

   Lists over 5,000 directories classified into 15 major classifications and more than 2,100 subject headings. Directory categories include industry, business, education, government, science, and public affairs.

4. *National Trade and Professional Associations of the United States*

   Columbia Books Inc., Publishers, 1350 New York Avenue, N.W., Suite 207, Washington, D.C. 20005

   Lists about 6,500 national trade associations; labor unions; professional, scientific, or technical societies; and other national organizations.

5. *Encyclopedia of Associations*

   Gale Research Company, Book Tower, Detroit, Michigan 48226.

   Lists over 1,200 trade and professional associations serving the U.S.

6. State Industrial Directories

Available at major libraries, state chambers of commerce, and state employment security offices. Provide a comprehensive listing of nearly every company that does business within the state. Each company is assigned a Standard Industrial Classification (S.I.C.) number; defines the product(s) manufactured.

7. Chamber of Commerce Directories

Many city and area chambers of commerce publish directories similar to the state industrial directories, but geographically restricted to areas they serve. These can normally be acquired at nominal cost.

During the research phase of your project, target companies can usually be identified using these reference sources. Most of the directories can be used to directly identify specific target companies. Others are used as resources to identify industrial and trade associations, from which membership directories can be acquired for a minimal fee. Many times target companies belong to such trade associations, and membership directories may be borrowed by simply contacting someone you know who is employed with one of these target companies.

With a day or two of good research using these sources, you can develop a comprehensive listing of target companies to be used as the basis for your mail campaign.

Identifying Target Executives

When preparing your mailing list, it is most important to identify not only the names of target companies but also the names and titles of specific executives and managers to whom your mailing will be sent. This type of pinpoint mailing is more likely to generate a positive response than one that is simply sent to a functional department within the organization.

When researching the names of target executives, there is one important rule to keep in mind: Don't send your mailing to the Personnel or Employment Department. These departments, although sometimes well-organized and highly professional, are not always aware of potential new openings that may develop. It is better to send your cover letter and résumé to a functional manager within the functional area for which you are applying. These persons are more keenly aware of the business problems and dynamics that can spawn the need for additional human resources, specific technical skills, etc. Sometimes the receipt of a well-prepared cover letter and résumé is just the thing that triggers the decision to hire. I have seen this happen time and time again.

When doing your research, try to identify the person in the organization who, by job title and organizational level, is likely to be the person to whom you would report if you were hired by this organization. Thus if you are a production manager, target the operations manager; if an operations manager, target the director of manufacturing; if a director of manufacturing, target the vice president of manufacturing; and so on. When job titles are confusing, and you are in doubt as to which position to pick, select the functional head of the area for which you are applying. If your mailing hits at too high an organizational level, chances are that it will be passed down to the right organizational level.

When you are in a more senior management position (i.e., senior manager, director, vice president), this part of the research can be fairly easy. Many industrial directories furnish the names and titles of persons at the director levels and above. When you are in a middle management, junior management, or professional level position, however, things are a bit tougher. In such cases you will need to dig a little harder and a little deeper to get the information that you need.

For these more junior level positions, the professional and trade association directories are useful sources of information. Many of these associations publish membership directories that list not only companies, but individual members as well. In many cases, these individual members are listed two ways: (1) Alphabetically, by last name, and (2) Alphabetically, under the name of the company with whom they are employed. Here is a process you can use to identify these people:

1. Use the *National Trade and Professional Associations of the United States* and the *Encyclopedia of Associations* as your key sources.

2. Identify the trade associations to which your target companies are likely to belong.

    a. Contact trade associations to determine if a membership directory is published.

    b. Determine if this directory lists the names and titles of individual members (in addition to company membership).

    c. Where individual memberships are listed, order copy of directory. (Note: If distribution of directory is limited to association members only, you will need to identify a member and borrow a copy. To facilitate this, ask for contact information on area officers.)

    d. Use these trade membership directories to identify the names and titles of target executives for the target firms that you have chosen for your mailing.

3. Using the same reference sources as for trade associations, identify the professional associations and societies to which your target executives are most likely to belong.

    a. Contact these professional associations to determine if a membership directory is published.

    b. Order copy of directory for research purposes.

    c. Research the names and titles of target executives using these directories.

4. Use the *Directory of Directories* to supplement search steps 1, 2, and 3 above.

   a. Obtain appropriate trade association and professional association membership directories.

   b. Research the names and titles of target executives using these directories.

If you have been fairly thorough and diligent with executing the steps of this research process, you will have been successful in identifying the names and titles of most target executives for the target firms that you are planning to include in your direct mail campaign. In those cases where you were not successful in identifying the specific person who occupies the organizational level targeted during your research, it is suggested that you forward your cover letter and résumé to the functional vice president for the functional area in which you have an interest. If you are in manufacturing, use the vice president or director of manufacturing as your target person for mailing purposes. Such persons are normally more easily identified using one of the major industrial directories (e.g., *Dun & Bradstreet Million Dollar Directory, Dun & Bradstreet Middle Market Directory, Poor's Register of Corporation Directors & Executives, Standard Directory of Advertisers*).

You have now concluded the research portion of your direct mail campaign and are ready to proceed with the mailing itself.

The Mailing

To increase the probability that your letter will actually be received and read by the person whom you have targeted, it is best to type each envelope on an individual basis. Avoid the use of address labels since this smacks of a mass mailing, and is likely to get snagged by your target's secretary, who is frequently trained in the process of screening out all junk mail from the boss' mail folder.

To get away from this mass mail look, it is advisable to use envelopes made of quality stock. It may cost a little more, but it creates a professional and personalized impression. As an additional step to improving the probability of readership, type the word CONFIDENTIAL on either the front or back of the envelope. In some cases, use of this word may cause your letter to pass unopened from the secretary directly to the targeted executive.

At this point you've done just about everything that you can do to design and execute an effective mail campaign. The next step is to sit back and see what it produces. Don't get your hopes up too high, since most experts say that such direct mail campaigns will usually generate not more than a two to five percent response rate. So for every 100 letters that you mail, you will probably get a response from only two to five companies. Quite frankly, in the employment market, you'll be doing very well to get this type of return. Keep in mind that it only takes one good inquiry to generate a job opportunity that is particularly attractive. So, hang in there! Your hard work might just pay off.

The next chapter deals with the subject of networking—a tried and proven technique for generating interview opportunities and job offers.

10

The Networking Process

Employment networking is by far the most highly touted job hunting technique used today. In recent years, this technique has gotten considerable play and, today, stands as the undisputed centerpiece of most, if not all, professional outplacement employment training programs. It is the one employment strategy that seems to have the unanimous support of both seasoned employment and outplacement professionals alike. The reason for this is simple: It works!

Although admittedly a very effective job search method, the single largest drawback of the networking process is that it demands a considerable investment of personal time and discipline to execute it properly. It is for this reason that employed persons, who don't have the luxury of the time and freedom of those who are unemployed, find it difficult to adopt as their primary job search strategy. This is not to say that networking has no place in the employed person's job hunting campaign. It does! It simply means that, due to the practical constraints of time, it will need to take a back seat to other job hunting techniques that are a little less demanding.

By contrast, however, unemployed persons should make the networking process the centerpiece of their job search program. If well-planned and executed, this process can be extremely effectual in surfacing job opportunities and interviews. With the proper investment of time and discipline, it has consistently proven to be a most valuable strategy.

What is employment networking? Who should use it? How does it work? What are the elements of the process? These, and other similar questions, will be answered in this chapter. In addition, this chapter will present you with a systematic, step-by-step method for implementing the employment networking process. If carefully followed, this process should prove very productive in your job hunting campaign.

WHAT IS EMPLOYMENT NETWORKING?

A networking, by definition, is a group of things that are integrated and connected together to form a whole. In a figurative sense, it means anything that traps or ensnares, such as a web or a net. In a social sense, the term network has come to mean a process by which one reaches out to integrate and connect a group of friends for the purpose of securing their united support. The thing that is captured or ensnared is their assistance and support.

The social definition seems to fit the meaning of employment networking rather well. Employment networking is a process by which one reaches out to a group of friends and acquaintances for their ongoing support during the job hunting process. They are asked to provide their direct support by providing job leads and referrals, in addition to arranging for introduction to others who can also provide such leads and introductions. As more and more people are pulled in, the greater is the probability that the result will be job leads that will lead to employment interviews, and finally offers of employment.

Actually, the networking process is a bit like cell division. In cell division, each parent cell divides into two cells. These cells then also divide into two more (total of four cells). Each of the resultant four cells then divide into two (total eight cells), and so on, as this process continues to explode at a rapid rate. It is also like the familiar chain letter, where each person copies the letter and gives it to five friends, who copy it and give it to five more friends, who copy it and give it to five more friends, etc. The outcome is a geometric progression where the number of contacts increase at an ever increasing rate.

The theory behind employment networking is somewhat similar and becomes a sort of geometric progression. By starting with a selected group of friends or acquaintances (say 50 or so), you ask them to help you identify a suitable job. Importantly, you also ask these same friends and acquaintances to provide you with the names of three to five of their friends whom you might contact to ask for their assistance. This second level group are then asked for their assistance, as well as the names of three to five of their acquaintances whom you might contact. Thus a geometric progression, much like cell division, is started and begins to grow at an increasing rate. Unlike cell division, however, the speed at which this progression grows is limited by your ability to contact all of the people who are identified by this process.

The beauty of this networking process is that you can start with a small group of friends and acquaintances and, with their cooperation, explode these contacts into several hundred in fairly short order. The initial group is known as the Level I or Primary Group. The group to whom this Primary Group refers you is the Level II or Secondary Group. The next group is called Level III, etc. History has shown that few jobs are ever found through the Level I contacts. Instead, most jobs are found at the second, third and fourth levels. Thus, these contacts and subsequent referrals become very important to the success of the employment networking process.

As these contacts continue to expand and grow, so does the size of the social support net that you are building. The larger this net becomes, the more people are out there helping you on an ongoing basis. Sooner or later as the network continues to grow, you will begin to find job opportunities that are of interest to you.

Yes, this process really works! I've seen it work time and time again. I have personally had the opportunity to observe numerous persons use this process with a very high rate of success. In fact, of those who I have observed using this process, I have yet to see one failure.

Besides the obvious expanding number of persons who comprise the support group created by the networking process, what are the other factors that contribute to the success of this technique? There is one factor that is thought to significantly account for the success of the networking process. This is known as the *hidden job market*. Let's examine the hidden job market concept, so that you can appreciate exactly why the networking process is so very successful.

THE HIDDEN JOB MARKET

The hidden job market is a concept that has been around for a long time. There have been a number of employment related articles and books that describe it in various ways; and there is generally a great deal of uniformity about what is said.

It is widely believed, and well supported by both private and independent studies, that a very high percentage of jobs that are filled in the United States are filled informally through personal contact, long before they have had the opportunity to be advertised in a newspaper, or listed with a search firm, or employment agency. In fact, depending on which study you choose to cite, it is believed that between 63.4 and 74.5 percent of all jobs are filled through the informal social networking process. Most authoritative sources place the figure at about 70 percent.

Stated differently, only about 30 percent of all job openings in the United States ever reach the general public and become known through recruitment advertising or employment consultants. This is a rather startling number when we think about the number of persons who rely on advertising and employment agencies as the mainstays of their job hunting process. By restricting themselves to these sources, such persons are missing out on 70 percent of the total job market, right from the start.

If you are in the process of planning your job hunting campaign, it would seem rather foolhardy to ignore a full 70 percent of the market. It is imperative that you pay particular attention to this hidden job market, and that you become intimately familiar with the informal networking process that has been successfully used by so many to access this important segment of the market.

Sometimes people have the impression that this is a market to which only the rich, powerful, or privileged have access. Nothing could be further from the truth. The fact that this segment of the market represents a full 70 percent, should certainly, in itself, convince you otherwise. What makes this a *hidden* job market has nothing to do with access. It simply means that although these jobs exist, they are not readily visible to the general public and, therefore, require a little extra work to flush them out.

The special method that is used to identify and access the jobs that comprise the hidden job market is the informal networking process. Simply put, through personal contact, people become aware of these newly created positions, interview, and are hired to fill them long before they become the subject of a classified ad, display ad, or an employment agency search.

If you are to successfully compete in this important segment of the job market, you must become skilled in the employment networking process. It is this process that provides you the wherewithal to access this valuable market segment. Remember, it represents 70 percent of the job market. It's well worth going after.

The balance of this chapter is designed to train you in the use of the employment networking process. You will walk through this process, step-by-step, and become thoroughly familiar with how it works. If you are an attentive student, this process will serve you extremely well, and will prove to be a major factor in your job search campaign.

RESEARCH PHASE

The first step in the employment networking process is the research phase. The purpose of this phase is twofold:

1. Identification of target companies
2. Identification of Level I contacts

You need to start by identifying the target industry or industries that are likely to have interest in your background, and in which, of course, you would like to be employed. In most cases this should be fairly simple and require little, if any, research.

Next, you will need to consider the geography in which you plan to conduct your search. Will you relocate anywhere in the United States? Will you relocate overseas? Do you have geographical preferences? How about geographical restrictions? These questions need to be answered before you begin listing companies on your target list that are located in geographical areas to which you are unwilling to move. So, carefully define the geographical boundaries of your target area.

Logically, as you have probably already guessed, the next step is to identify the firms within your preferred industry segment and geographical target area, for whom you would like to work. This list of firms becomes your target list.

It is now time to develop your Level I contacts, which will serve to form the nucleus of your networking process. To begin this, make a list of persons whom you know. At this point, don't worry whether they have firsthand knowledge of your target industry or firms. Put each of their names, addresses, and telephone numbers on a three by five index card. Try to generate a list of over 100 of these Level I contacts. To help stimulate your thinking, here is a list of categories from which such contacts could come:

Fellow workers	Salespersons	Consultants
Past bosses	Relatives	Church
Barber	Accountant	Stockbroker
Professional associations	Trade associations	Alumnae associations
Past subordinates	Fraternity	Sorority
Club members	Neighbors	Teachers
Former classmates	Doctor	Dentist
Insurance agent	Lawyer	Banker
Pastor	Priest	Friends
Competitors	Customers	Clients
Military	Government	Editors
Scouting	Sports	Hobbies
Commuting	Grocer	Butcher

Having reviewed these categories and developed as many contact names as possible, sort your index cards into two categories:

1. Those who could potentially know persons in your target industry

2. Those who are less likely to know such persons

You are now ready to begin the process of contacting these Level I contacts and starting the employment networking process.

MAKING LEVEL I CONTACTS

Level I contacts are, for the most part, persons you know. Although you may at first feel somewhat shy about contacting them and asking for their help, remember the following:

1. Most people really are quite willing to help others, if approached in the right way.

2. Most people feel complimented by a request for advice and counsel. They are frequently pleased that you respect their knowledge enough to seek their counsel.

3. If unemployed, most people will be very understanding. With so many corporations going through downsizing programs, it is no longer a stigma to be unemployed. Additionally, many of the persons with whom you will be talking may have some concerns about their own job security, and are thus quite willing to help. After all, they could well be needing your help at some future point in time.

When contacting these Level I persons, you have the following objectives:

1. Make them aware of your job search.

2. Briefly acquaint them with your background and the type of job you seek.

3. Determine if they are aware of job openings that might be appropriate.

4. If not, ask them to suggest the names of persons who may know of such openings.

5. Determine if they would be willing to arrange a personal introduction to such persons.

6. If not, ask them for permission to use their name when contacting these persons.

7. Ask if they would mind if you send them a copy of your résumé. (Objective here is to further acquaint them with your background and make it possible for them to provide a copy of your résumé to others).

When calling these contacts, it is very important that you not ask them for a job. You don't want to do anything that would put them on the spot or cause embarrassment. It is best, therefore, to take a more indirect approach. Tell them that you are not asking them for a job, but are simply calling them to ask for assistance and advice in your job hunting campaign. When approached in this manner, most persons are quite willing to help and will do so, provided you give them the opportunity.

Remember, your goal is not only to identify job opportunities, but also to secure the names of referrals who will help expand your networking process. In each case, you should set a goal of acquiring the names of three to five contacts from each personal contact you make. Try to focus these referrals such that they will have contacts in your key target industries, or in the business function in which you have an employment interest.

When garnering the names of new referrals, make sure to transfer this information to an index card immediately. Record not only name, address, and phone number; but also the name of the source of the referral. In addition, if your source was unusually helpful, be sure to send a short *thank you* along with the copy of your résumé. Acknowledge your appreciation for his or her assistance in your job hunting campaign.

LEVEL II CONTACTS

Telephone contacts with your Level II Group should be handled somewhat differently from those in the Level I or Primary Group. In all cases, those who you contacted in the Level I or Primary Group were persons you personally know. Those in your Level II Group, however, are persons you have never met or, at best, may have met only briefly. For the most part, these Secondary or Level II contacts will fall into one of two categories:

1. Those either employed or having good personal contacts in your target industry

2. Those not employed or having direct contacts in your target industry.

Those falling into the first of these categories usually warrant a personal meeting, when this can be arranged. Their contacts are particularly valuable and could be extremely helpful to your networking process and overall job hunting campaign. You will want them, if possible, to be a part of your job search campaign, to actively work on your behalf to open doors, to arrange appropriate introductions to key persons within your target firms. There is nothing that can compare to a personal meeting when it comes to getting someone truly involved in helping you with your job hunting campaign. Here are the steps you should follow when trying to set up a meeting by phone:

1. Introduce yourself.

2. Explain that (*name of person making referral*) referred you to him/her and suggested that he/she could be of help to you in your job hunting campaign.

3. Explain that you are not asking for a job, but since he/she is knowledgeable of the industry, you would appreciate the

opportunity to meet, in order to get some ideas on how to best approach the industry as far as your job search is concerned.

4. If not possible to arrange a meeting, ask if he/she could take a few moments on the phone to be of some assistance. (Most will agree or, if not convenient, will offer to call back.)

5. Briefly describe your background and job search objective.

6. Ask if he/she is aware of any companies that may currently be looking for someone with your profile.

7. If so, ask for the names and titles of contacts he/she may have in these companies.

8. Ask if an introduction could be arranged.

9. If no introduction is possible, ask if you may use his/her name in making contact with these persons.

10. If not aware of anyone who is looking for someone with your profile, ask for the names of persons he/she knows who have contacts in this industry and may know persons having such openings. (Try to get the names of three to five such contacts.)

11. Ask if he/she would be willing to arrange a personal introduction.

12. If no personal introduction is possible, ask permission to use this person's name when contacting these referrals.

13. Ask if he/she would mind if you would send him/her a copy of your résumé. (Remember to include a thank-you letter along with your résumé.)

Should you be successful in arranging a personal meeting with one of these Level II contacts, in addition to the items mentioned above, you should include the following items in your agenda:

1. Ask him/her to review your résumé. Ask for thoughts and ideas on how it might be improved. (The objective here is to familiarize others with your background and qualifications).

2. Describe your job hunting strategy. Ask for thoughts and ideas as to how it could be made more effective.

3. Ask for an assessment of the industry. What segments and which companies are expanding? What segments are contracting?

4. What are some of the key issues and challenges currently faced by the industry? How might your background prove helpful?

In all cases, be sure to request the names of additional contacts in the field. This is your lifeline to a successful networking process. Without these key contacts, your campaign will lose its momentum and may eventually stall completely. This is something you can't afford to have happen. So be sure to keep the pipeline flowing with new names.

Contacts with Level III, Level IV, etc., groups should all be handled in much the same way as described here with the Level II Group.

GENERAL COMMENTS

As you can see, the employment networking process requires considerable time and effort to sustain it. It is a process that requires a great deal of organization and discipline in order to successfully carry it out. There is little question, however, that if you stick with it, the end results will prove well worth the expenditure of time.

Through your persistence and evergrowing network of valuable contacts, sooner or later you will find the position that you are searching for. With 70 percent of the job market at stake, it will definitely be a worthwhile investment of your time and effort.

11

Effective Interviewing

When preparing for the employment interview, there are a number of things that you can do to substantially improve your chances of success. Unfortunately, few persons invest the necessary time and energy into such preparation, and the result is often a mediocre showing. Generally, most people feel there is little if anything they can do to improve their overall interview skills and, thus, let the chips fall where they may. Never could they be more wrong!

If willing to invest the necessary time and effort, there is quite a bit that can be done to improve interview skills and positively affect the outcome of the employment interview. There is much you can do to anticipate the kinds of questions you will be asked, thus allowing you the opportunity to prepare better answers that will showcase your skills and set you apart from your competition. Besides this mechanical preparation, there are also some things that you can do from a strategic standpoint to enhance your candidacy. There is also the matter of advance research which, if done properly, can provide you with many clues necessary to formulate a winning interview plan and strategy.

This chapter is designed to help you to systematically plan and execute an interview strategy that will provide you with substantial competitive advantage, and dramatically improve the probability for a successful result.

HOW EMPLOYERS THINK

Important insight can be gained, when preparing for the employment interview, by forcing yourself to think much the same as the employer would.

During the employment interview, the employer's main focus is usually on the candidate's ability to solve key problems and to perform specific job functions. The technical knowledge and skills needed to solve these problems and perform these key functions become the central point of the job interview. These knowledge and skill factors become the selection criteria against which the candidate's qualifications are gauged by the employer during the interview discussion. They comprise the *technical* or *can-do* part of the interview.

Interestingly, it is the technical or can-do portion of the interview with which employers are most preoccupied. In fact, it is estimated that in the typical interview the average employer will spend 75 to 85 percent of the total interview time exploring the candidate's technical qualifications for the position. This is an important statistic to keep in mind when it comes to interview preparation. It suggests that a similar portion of your interview preparation time should be committed to this same area.

Why is this the case? Why is it that employers spend so much time on technical qualifications rather than other important dimensions of a candidate's overall capability? There are several probable reasons:

1. Technical qualifications are more apparent and, therefore, more easily defined.

2. Technical qualifications are less abstract and are thus more easily measured.

3. Most interviewers are better trained in interviewing for technical qualifications, so are more comfortable in this area.

4. For a manager, there is a tendency to think in terms of the key technical problems that need to be solved. These are the issues foremost in his/her mind.

5. Most managers have had little or no training in techniques for measuring more abstract selection criteria (e.g., motivation or organizational fit). They feel less comfortable in these areas, therefore, and will tend to shy away or de-emphasize such categories.

Although devoting considerably less time to this category, the second major area on which employers will focus during the employment interview is the area of employee motivation. Unlike technical credentials, which are the *can-do* aspects of a candidate's qualifications, the motivation area is the *will-do* dimension of selection. A candidate may be technically qualified and able to perform the job, but is he or she sufficiently interested and motivated to actually do the job (or to do it well)? Most employers understand this subtle difference and attempt to gain some insight into candidate motivation during the interview discussion.

Because of the abstract nature of motivation, most interviewers will make some basic observations about the candidate in this area, but will not commit much interview time to doing so. Fundamental questions about the candidate's interest in the position and general work ethic may surface during the interview, but few interviewers are adequately prepared to probe this area much more deeply than this. It is estimated that only about 10 to 15 percent of total interview time is committed to investigating the motivation or can-do factors.

Although employers seldom think of it in these terms, the final area of employer focus during the employment interview is organizational compatibility (i.e., how well the individual will fit into the organization's culture). Again, due to the abstract nature of this concept, attempts by the employer to measure organizational compatibility are, for the most part, fairly shallow and seem to center around a rather vague notion of liking or not liking the candidate. Although specific reasons frequently remain undefined, there is some feeling generated during the interview about the candidate's ability to fit in.

Although clearly a factor in employee selection, the notion of organizational compatibility is an area where most interviewers feel, perhaps, least prepared to measure a candidate's qualifications through specific interview techniques. Simply put, most employers don't really know what kind of questions to ask in order to examine this important area more thoroughly. As a consequence, very little interview time is ever committed to asking questions concerning organizational compatibility (probably less than five percent). As a candidate, however, it is important to be aware that although employers may invest little if any direct interview time in exploring this area specifically, you can be sure that employers will, nonetheless, make some very real (if not potentially inaccurate) observations about your organizational fit.

Thus, it would appear that in order to prepare yourself for an effective interview, it is necessary for you to think as the employer and to spend some time focusing on the three main areas:

1. Technical qualifications (The can-do factors)

2. Motivational qualifications (The will-do factors)

3. Organizational compatibility

This is exactly where you can expect the employer to focus during interview discussions.

Knowing this, how can you prepare in advance of the interview to effectively address these focal points? What sorts of questions should you anticipate being asked, and how can you be ready to answer them?

The next few pages of this chapter systematically explore each of these interview areas so that you can anticipate how the employer will approach them and know what to expect. Furthermore, there are specific methods and suggestions for better preparing yourself to address these important areas. The balance of the chapter discusses various other interviewing strategies and techniques for improving your overall interviewing effectiveness.

TECHNICAL QUALIFICATIONS

How does one go about determining the technical qualifications for a given position in advance of the interview? The logical answer to this is, "Through position analysis." Consider, for a moment, the process that the employer typically goes through when determining these same technical criteria.

Typically, when an employer begins the process of developing candidate selection criteria for use in the interview, the first step is to review certain key documents relating to both the position as well as the department in which the position is located. This usually includes such things as the job description, department business plan, department objectives, and specific business objectives.

While reviewing these documents, the employer attempts to determine the key functions and responsibilities of the position, and then translates these into the technical qualifications felt to be essential to good job performance.

Although you may not have all of these documents available to you, in most cases it is possible to secure a copy of the job description from the employer in advance of the interview. Most employers will provide a copy of this document just for the asking. Having obtained a copy of the job description, you should go through the same type of position analysis that the employer will likely go through in translating the requirements of the position into candidate qualifications. Use the following questions to complete this job analysis:

1. What are the key functions for which this position is accountable?

   _____

   _____

   _____

   _____

2. Which of these functions are most important to job success?

   _____

   _____

   _____

   _____

3. In which of these functions is it essential that the candidate have experience? How much and what kind?

   _____

   _____

   _____

   _____

4. What are the principal, ongoing responsibilities of this position (i.e., the ongoing results expected of the job)?

_____

_____

_____

_____

5. What technical knowledge and skills are needed by the candidate to achieve these required results on an ongoing basis?

_____

_____

_____

_____

6. What are the key technical issues and problems to be solved by the incumbent in this position?

_____

_____

_____

_____

7. What technical knowledge and skills must a candidate have to successfully solve these problems and address these issues?

_____

_____

_____

_____

8. What level and type of formal education is likely required to equip a candidate to successfully handle the technical aspects of this position?

_____

_____

_____

_____

As with the employer, by answering these or similar questions you should be able to delineate a list of technical or can-do qualifications important to successful job performance. These qualifications can normally be classified into the following categories:

Formal Education

The level and type of formal education needed for successful job performance

Functional Experience

The level and type of experience required in specific functional areas

Technical Capability

The technical knowledge and skills needed to solve the key problems and meet the major technical challenges of the position.

SELF EVALUATION

Modern interview theory is based upon the concept that the best predictor of future behavior is past behavior. To put it differently, if you want to forecast how well a person will do carrying out a certain function or solving a certain kind of problem, find out how well he or she did tackling similar things in the past. If results were good in the past, there is some basis for believing that they will be equally as good in the future. This type of behavioral interviewing is becoming very popular today and is in fairly widespread use.

In order to prepare for a behavioral interview (which, by the way, is an excellent way to prepare for almost any type interview), you will need to systematically analyze your past experience in search of evidence that you have, and can apply, the technical knowledge and skills that are required for successful performance of your desired position. It is no longer enough to simply state that you meet these requirements; you must be prepared to demonstrate this from the results you have achieved in the past. The closer these examples are to current issues and problems faced by the employer, the more convinced the employer will be that you have the necessary skills and technical capability to perform well in the position for which you will be interviewing.

In order to simplify this process and save considerable time, refer to the historical information that you prepared from Chapter 4 of this book. You will recall that, in assembling this data, you were required to furnish a list of responsibilities and accomplishments for each of your past positions. This information is an excellent basis for systematically reviewing your past background for evidence of the technical knowledge and skills currently sought by the interviewer. The questions listed below should prove helpful in sifting out relevant information as you go along.

One of the advantages to using this approach is that this same information served as the basis for preparing your résumé. So, much of this information is probably already contained in your résumé, and the interviewer's attention can be drawn to this fact as the interview progresses.

Key Questions for Self-Evaluation

1. In which of your past positions were you accountable for the same (or similar) functional areas as required for this position?

   _____

   _____

_____

_____

2. What functions were they, and what was the nature of your accountability?

_____

_____

_____

_____

3. With which of these required functions have you had little or no experience?

_____

_____

_____

_____

4. In such cases, what (if any) experience have you had in related functional areas that might be considered equivalent experience?

_____

_____

_____

_____

5. In which of your past positions have you had the same or similar principal, ongoing responsibilities as required by this position?

_____

_____

_____

6. What were the key technical problems that you were required to solve in order to meet these principal, ongoing responsibilities?

_____

_____

_____

_____

7. How well did you do? What key problems were solved? What important results were achieved?

Key Problems: _____

_____

_____

Important Results: _____

_____

_____

8. What key technical problems and issues did you face in past jobs that were the same (or similar) to the issues and problems you will face in the new position?

_____

_____

_____

_____

9. How well did you do? What key problems or issues did you resolve? What important results did you achieve?

Key Problems: _____

_____

_____

Important Results: _____

_____

_____

10. In what ways do these results demonstrate the technical knowledge and skills sought by the prospective employer?

_____

_____

_____

_____

11. What does this analysis tell you about your overall qualifications to successfully meet the technical challenges of the new position?

_____

_____

_____

_____

12. What relevant major problems are you likely to be able to solve for your new employer? With what probable results?

Relevant Problems: _____

_____

_____

Probable Results: _____

_____

_____

13. What evidence can you cite to substantiate this capability?

_____

_____

_____

_____

_____

14. Where are your shortfalls? What key technical problems are you likely not to be able to solve in the new position?

_____

_____

_____

_____

15. What specific technical knowledge or skills do you lack that would account for this lack of capability?

_____

_____

_____

_____

16. What steps are you prepared to take in order to acquire this knowledge or skills?

_____

_____

_____

_____

17. How will you manage this part of the job while you acquire the needed capability?

_____

_____

_____

_____

As you can see, working hard to answer these questions is an excellent exercise to prepare you for the forthcoming interview. It focuses your attention on those aspects of the job most likely to be of interest to the prospective employer. In addition, it prepares you to quickly cite convincing evidence of your overall ability to perform key elements of the job.

This exercise thoroughly prepares you to discuss specific knowledge and skills necessary to good job performance and to also cite behavioral evidence that objectively supports your professional competence in these critical areas. Such vigorous preparation will clearly improve your interview results and provide you with a substantial competitive advantage over those with whom you may need to compete.

MOTIVATIONAL QUALIFICATIONS

As previously stated in this chapter, motivational qualifications mean those personal characteristics necessary to achieve the key results necessary to good job performance. It is the drive, energy and desire to accomplish these results. It is one thing to have the technical qualifications to perform the responsibilities of the job. It is quite another to be motivated to do the work. Without such motivation key results will not be achieved and there will be performance failure.

When attempting to measure these motivational factors, employers will ask certain questions and will also observe candidate behavior for signs of interest or disinterest. Seasoned interviewers will be particularly alert to the candidate's body language, which can often telegraph the candidate's interest in (and motivation to perform) the work.

Here are some key questions that the employer may use to assess your interest and motivation to perform the job:

1. How do you feel about this position?

2. What aspect of the job most interests you? Why?

3. What aspect of the job least interests you? Why?

4. How would you rate your overall interest in this position? Why?

5. Which of your past positions did you like most? Why?

6. Which of your past positions did you like least? Why?

7. Which of these past positions most resembles this new position? In what ways?

8. What factors must be present to make a job interesting and exciting for you?

9. What factors would make a job less interesting and exciting?

10. Which of these factors are present in this job?

11. What aspects of this job are you likely to perform best? Why?

12. What aspects of this job are you likely to perform least well? Why?

13. On a scale of one to ten (ten, high), where would you rate the level of your interest in this position?

14. How might you change this job to make it more interesting and exciting?

15. What concerns do you have about this job? Why?

You also need to pay particular attention to your body language during the interview. For maximum effectiveness, you want to appear alert, interested, and relatively enthusiastic throughout the interview process. Here are some clues about body language that should help you as an interviewee:

1. Sit up relatively straight (but not rigid) in your chair. Good posture can convey a feeling of positive energy and an increased

level of interest in the conversation. It can also suggest that you are a person who is alert, attentive, and interested in the ideas of others.

2. Never lay back or slouch in your chair. This may suggest that you are lazy, sloppy, careless, inattentive, or disinterested.

3. Acknowledge key points made by your host with a nod, smile, or other appropriate gesture that suggests you are attentive and responsive to the conversational topic.

4. Good eye contact with the interviewer is important throughout the interview. In addition to telegraphing your attentiveness, eye contact conveys that you are sensitive, open, forthright, secure, self-confident, and comfortable in your relationship with others.

5. To the contrary, poor eye contact may suggest that you are inattentive, disinterested, shifty, uncertain, unsure, self-conscious, shy, and ill-at-ease in your interpersonal relations.

6. Avoid nervous habits such as tapping your pencil or fingers, pulling your ear lobes, rubbing your nose, playing with your tie, stroking your hair. These habits are very distracting and detract from your presentation. In addition, such actions suggest that you are nervous, high-strung, intense, insecure, and generally uncomfortable with others.

7. Avoid crossing your arms in front of you. To some, this may indicate that you are defensive, unfriendly, and prefer to keep others at a distance.

Body language can, and does, have a very real impact on interview results. In particular, it can transmit strong messages to the employer concerning your motivation, drive, energy, desire, and general interest level. Seasoned interviewers will closely observe your behavior and body language throughout the interview discussion for signs of your level of interest and motivation to perform the job.

During the interview, you should be alert for opportunities to demonstrate your motivation and confirm your interest in the position. Be sure to verbally express your interest and demonstrate your enthusiasm as the opportunity presents itself. Here are a few statements and phrases that can help accomplish this:

1. That sounds very interesting!

2. I have always particularly liked doing _____!

3. That sounds exciting and challenging!

4. I think I could do that quite well!

5. That's an area where I feel I could make some meaningful contributions.

6. I have some ideas on how to approach that issue.

7. Here's how I would approach that.

8. I feel that kind of work is challenging and exciting!

9. I've always been fascinated by _____.

10. I would enjoy doing that!

11. That sounds challenging and stimulating!

12. I have always had a strong interest in _____.

13. I feel I could make some real contributions to _____.

14. I would welcome the challenge of doing _____.

15. That's an exciting area—one that is continually challenging and interesting to me.

Don't pass up the opportunity to express your interest and desire for the position at the conclusion of the interview. If you are really interested in the job, tell your host of your interest. Tell him or her that you have enjoyed your interview, and that it has served to heighten your interest in the position. Briefly summarize key areas of the job that sound particularly attractive. Voice your confidence that you can perform well in the position, and that you have a strong interest. Here is an example of something you might say:

Mr. Jones, I have enjoyed the day. Although I was already interested in this position, today's discussions have heightened this interest. I would enjoy doing _____, _____ and _____; and feel these are areas where I could make a strong contribution to the ABC Company. In many ways, this position seems like a good fit for my experience, skills, and capabilities. I hope the ABC Company will elect to pursue this further. I look forward to hearing from you.

Thus, by demonstrating your interest and enthusiasm for the position, both verbally and through body language, you suggest to the employer that you are well-motivated to perform successfully in the job. Interest and enthusiasm convey that you have the necessary drive, energy, and desire to accomplish the objectives and results. You satisfy not only the technical or can-do requirements of the position, but also the motivational or will-do requirements, as well. This leaves only the matter of organizational compatibility.

ORGANIZATIONAL COMPATIBILITY

As mentioned earlier in this chapter, employers are usually not well versed in measuring this factor. They will, nevertheless, make some judgements about your organizational compatibility. How well do your ideas and philosophy align with that of the organization? How well do your style and personality fit with the other members of the group with whom you will be working? These are concerns that will be on the employer's mind, and you will want to be aware of this as you prepare for your interview discussion.

Interviewers who are more seasoned and skillful than others may attempt to probe this area. If they do, here are some of the questions that you might anticipate:

1. How would you describe yourself? What adjectives would you use?

2. How have your past bosses described you? What have they said when describing you?

ง would you describe your operating style? What is char-
ristic about the way in which you operate?

4. ᵣᵢₒw would you describe the type of environment in which you enjoy working? What is characteristic of that environment?

5. Of the various environments in which you have worked, which did you most enjoy? Why? What was present in that environment?

6. Of the various environments in which you have worked, which did you least enjoy? Why? What was present that accounted for your dissatisfaction?

7. What is your business philosophy? What do you believe is important to having a successful operation?

8. What type of business philosophy do you find least agreeable? What do you feel makes such a philosophy less effective?

9. With what kind of people do you most enjoy working? What is characteristic about such people?

10. How would you categorize the kind of people with whom you least enjoy associating?

Other than being aware of these potential questions and thinking about how you will want to respond to them, there is probably very little that you can do to prepare for this area. At the time of the interview, however, there are some things that you can do, in a strategic sense, to stack the deck somewhat in your favor. Here are a few pointers:

1. During the interview, be particularly alert to the environment around you.

2. Make careful observations about the kind of people that you meet.

3. In what ways are these people similar?

4. In what ways are they different?

5. What observations can you make about their personal styles?

6. Are there some common attributes (e.g., conservative, liberal, risk-taking, entrepreneurial, careful, analytical, etc.)?

7. What observations can you make about their operating styles? Are there some general conformities?

8. What is the overriding management style and philosophy?

9. What is characteristic about the leaders of the group?

10. In what ways are they similar (i.e., personality, operating style, philosophy, etc.)?

11. In what ways are they different (i.e., personal characteristics, operating style, business philosophy, etc.)?

Observations of this type can prove very helpful in understanding the organizational culture and environment. The data that you collect through this process can be very helpful in guiding your answers to the questions that the employer may ask, as outlined previously. For example, if your observations suggest that this is a very conservative, analytical group that values good planning and analytical skills, you don't want to come across as a highly creative risk-taker, who likes to make quick decisions and get on with the action. Clearly, you would be a mismatch and would not be seen as compatible with the group. Nothing will scuttle your chances faster!

A word of caution, however, at this juncture. Although these strategies may improve your competitive edge in winning the interview, it may not be the best thing for your career. It would be most irresponsible of me not to draw this to your attention. What good is it to win the interview if the end result is going to require you to work in an environment in which you will be unhappy? Sooner or later, this unhappiness will result in your personal isolation and reflect in your performance.

If you are incompatible with the culture and organizational environment of the company with which you are interviewing, move on to your next target company and next set of interviews as soon as possible. Why risk unhappiness, and possibly your career, when the odds are decidedly against you?

We have now thoroughly covered the topics of technical qualifications (the can-do factors), motivation (the will-do factors), and organizational compatibility (organizational fit). You have been given a step-by-step process and methodology for thoroughly preparing yourself for these three important areas of the job interview. If you have invested the necessary time and effort in these exercises, you will have substantially improved your interview skills and readiness, and assured yourself of a strong competitive advantage in the interview process. Few, if any candidates, will be better prepared for this important test.

Beyond this tedious mechanical preparation, there are some strategic things that you can do to additionally strengthen your competitive position. The balance of this chapter is devoted to discussion of some strategies that can further help your cause.

ADVANCE KNOWLEDGE — CANDIDATE SPECIFICATION

The term *candidate specification* is used by employment professionals to describe the document that is prepared by the employer to describe the qualifications needed for successful performance in the position. This candidate specification normally consists of a list of specific knowledge, skills, and experience that the employer feels are essential to successful performance of the technical aspects of the job. It may also describe the personal style and attributes thought to be important to job success. In most companies, this specification is reduced to writing, and is passed along to both the employment department, as well as the members of the interview team, who will be involved in the interview and selection process.

Having access to this candidate specification in advance of the interview, is analogous to having a copy of the final exam in advance of the test date. It gives you an opportunity to study and prepare, thus substantially improving the probability of doing well and achieving high marks. Knowing the contents of this candidate specification in advance, will provide you with a bird's-eye view of the specific selection criteria to be used by the employer in candidate evaluation. This will allow you to anticipate the kinds of questions you are likely to be asked, and will substantially improve the probability of a favorable outcome.

So, what can you do to secure this information in advance of the interview? The answer is simple—*just ask for it!* You shouldn't expect that someone will give you a written copy; instead, ask for a verbal description of these requirements.

Strategically speaking, the best time to ask for a description of the candidate specification is at the time you are first contacted by the employer. It is at this time that the balance of power is in your favor, and you have the greatest leverage to extract this vital information from the employer. Since, at this point, the employer is intent on selling you on the idea of an employment interview, you are in the unique position to extract some key information which, at other times, may be difficult to elicit. To make the most of this opportunity, it is suggested that you employ the following methodology:

1. Tell the employer that, although the position sounds somewhat interesting, you would appreciate a little more

information to help you decide whether you would like to pursue the matter further.

2. Ask for a description of the key functional responsibilities of the position.

3. Which of these does he/she consider to be most important to job success?

4. What are the key problems and challenges with which you will be faced?

5. In what areas is the company looking for major improvement?

6. What education, functional experience, knowledge, and skills is he/she seeking in a candidate?

7. Which of these is considered most important?

8. What is there about your background that interests him/her?

9. Ask for a mailed copy of the job description.

10. Assuming you are interested at this point, thank the employer for the information and say that you would like to accept the interview invitation.

Be careful not to push for too much information at this point, since this strategy could backfire. If the employer begins to stiffen and you sense that you are either pushing too hard or are simply asking for too much, back off. Continuing to push for more information could work to your disadvantage by implying that you are too pushy, overly cautious, indecisive, or lacking in self-confidence.

If you are successful in your endeavor, however, you have pulled off an important strategic coup. Since you now have a thorough understanding of the employer's requirements and priorities, you are in an excellent position to know what aspects of your background and qualifications are likely to be of greatest interest.

Strategically, this provides you with considerable advantage over potential competition by allowing you to emphasize and showcase those skills and abilities of greatest interest to the employer.

THE PERFORMANCE IMPROVEMENT STRATEGY

The basic objective of the performance improvement strategy is for you to establish yourself as someone who can solve the ongoing problems faced by the employer, and thus bring about improved organizational performance. In my book, *The Five Minute Interview*, I refer to this as the *voids* strategy.

In order to effectuate this strategy, you must first determine performance voids in the current organization. What aspects of the current position, in the opinion of the hiring manager (the one to whom you would report), could be better performed? This, and similar questions, need to be answered during the early stages of the interview discussion so that you will be able to have time to think and carefully formulate a strategy that will allow you to position yourself as someone who can effectively address these deficits and contribute to the improved effectiveness of the organization.

Here are some good questions that you can employ early in the interview to identify these employment voids, and provide you with the kind of information that will help you to effectively carry out this strategy:

1. In your judgement, what areas of the current job could be better performed?

2. What kind of improvement would you like to see in these areas? Why?

3. Which of these areas would you most like to see improved?

4. Why is improvement in this area of particular interest to you?

5. What kind of improvement would you like to see?

6. Are there key, ongoing responsibilities of this position not currently being met? What are they?

7. Which of these, if any, do you feel are important? Why?

8. What factors have hindered performance of these responsibilities? Why?

9. What major changes and improvements would you most like to see brought about by a new incumbent? Why?

10. What type of improvement would you like to see?

11. What major barriers and obstacles stand in the way of realizing this improvement?

Answers to these questions will provide you with some ideas of the kinds of changes and improvements that the new boss would like to see brought to the organization. By demonstrating your willingness and ability to tackle these areas, and by citing evidence of similar problems you have successfully tackled in the past, you will position yourself as someone who will bring change and improvement to the organization. Most importantly, such improvement is in areas the hiring manager personally considers essential to organization effectiveness.

If carefully executed, this can prove to be an effective strategy. It creates the impression that you are someone who is focused on bringing change and improvement to the organization. In this sense, it suggests that you are someone who is willing to go beyond the traditional boundaries of the job, someone who will reach out in an effort to add value to the organization.

THE STRATEGIC CHANGE AGENT

Another key strategy that you can employ to increase your interviewing effectiveness is that of positioning yourself as a *strategic change agent*—one who can effectuate cultural change and achieve the important results essential to realization of the company's strategic mission and goals. In the lingo of the executive search profession, this is what is known as *a force*.

Although always in demand, the popularity and demand for strategic change agents has intensified in recent years. In the last few years, with intensified competition from foreign competition, many U.S. firms and industries have been in a survival mode. The intensity of this competition is forcing these organizations to accelerate culture change at a rate that has never before been seen. U.S. corporations are beginning to set very high goals for major improvement in such critical areas as increased employee productivity, higher quality, and reduced costs. These changes need to be sufficiently great to rival the Japanese and Koreans, and guarantee the long term survival and growth of the American free enterprise system.

These cultural changes have had significant impact on the interview and selection process. Generally, most employers are looking for candidates who have a proclivity to strategic change. They no longer need people who can come in and perform the job. Instead, they are looking for those who will change the job, those who will reach out and push the barriers of traditional job performance, those who will bring productive change and improvement, those who will be "value adding" to the organization.

The key to this interview strategy is knowing what change it is that the employer wishes to bring about. Your strategy needs to be aligned with the strategic goals of the organization if it is going to be perceived as value adding. Effective implementation of this strategy requires that you have a good understanding of the strategic goals and objectives of the organization. Here are some good questions to use at the beginning of the interview to flush this important information out:

1. What are the key strategic goals and objectives of the organization?

2. What are the major changes that are necessary to achieve these goals and objectives?

3. What effect will these changes have on the department or function for which I will be working?

4. What new results will be expected?

5. What current responsibilities will continue?

6. What current responsibilities will become obsolete?

7. Considering these changes, what new skills and capabilities do you feel will be necessary to ensure future job performance?

8. Which of these qualifications will be most important? Why?

9. Which of these will be least important? Why?

You will note that these questions have been designed to help the job candidate to define not only the key strategic changes that the employer desires, but also to define the important skills and capabilities that the employer feels are vital to future performance success.

As with performance improvement strategy, these questions should be asked early in the interview discussion so that you will be able to have time to think and formulate your strategy. To be effective, this strategy will require that you emphasize your skills and capabilities to drive strategic change, and realize the strategic goals and objectives of the company. You need to position yourself as someone who can drive these changes, realize the desired results and add strategic value to the organization. This establishes you as someone who is capable of going considerably beyond the traditional boundaries of the current job, someone who will drive positive change, someone who is truly capable of adding significant value to the organization, someone who will provide the company with the ability to achieve its future objectives and accomplish its strategic mission.

COMMON INTERVIEW QUESTIONS

You have now been exposed to several interviewing strategies that can provide immeasurable assistance to your overall effectiveness in the interview process. Being prepared with interviewing strategies alone will not guarantee an effective interview. In addition to this preparation, you will also need to fine tune your actual interviewing skills. More specifically, you will need to be prepared to sufficiently answer a wide variety of penetrating questions that are likely to be asked during the interview.

It would be impossible for any book to list all of the questions that could possibly be asked in the course of an employment interview. The array of possible choices is just too enormous. There are too many variables (e.g., organizations, industries, occupations, skills, etc.) to make this a practical consideration. It is only possible, therefore, to select a sampling of interview questions that are felt to be representative of the kinds that you are likely to encounter. The following questions, in addition to being fairly common, are also among the more difficult and thought-provoking. They should prove a good warm up exercise for helping to fine tune your interviewing skills.

Early Background

These are representative of the questions that might be asked concerning your childhood and family background:

1. Tell me about your early childhood.

2. What major events occurred during your childhood that had the greatest impact on your life?

3. In what ways did these help to shape your life?

4. How would you describe your early family life?

5. What important values did you acquire during your early years?

6. How have these affected your life?

7. Who most influenced you during your early years?

8. What impact did this person have on you?

9. What do you consider to be your most significant accomplishments while growing up?

10. Why were they significant?

Education

1. What were your reasons for choosing _____ college?

2. What were the factors that led to your decision to select _____ as a major?

3. How did your college education prepare you for life?

4. How did your college education prepare you for your current career?

5. What were your most significant accomplishments in college?

6. Why were they significant?

7. What kind of a student were you?

8. How might you have improved your effectiveness as a student?

9. What were your favorite courses? Why?

10. Which courses did you like least? Why?

11. How did you make use of your spare time?

12. What leadership roles did you assume while on campus?

13. How effective were you as a leader?

14. What results demonstrate your effectiveness as a leader?

15. What did you learn as a leader?

Work Experience

1. How did you decide to select _____ as a career?

2. What were the factors that most influenced this decision?

3. Of the past positions that you have held, which did you like most? Why?

4. Which past position did you like least? Why?

5. What were the factors that led to your decision to join _____ company?

6. What were the events and factors that led to your departure from _____ company?

7. What were your most important contributions and accomplishments in your position as _____ with _____ company?

8. How would you compare your position as _____ with _____ company to your position as _____ with _____ company?

9. Which of these positions did you like most? Why?

10. Which of these positions did you enjoy least? Why?

11. If we were to contact your current boss for a reference, what would he say about you?

12. What would he describe as your strengths? Why?

13. What areas would be identified as needing improvement? Why?

14. What are you doing to improve these areas?

15. What could you do to improve your overall performance in your current position?

16. What do you like most about your current job? Why?

17. What do you like least about your current job? Why?

18. What major projects have you undertaken in your current job that are beyond those normally required for this position?

19. How satisfied have you been with your career progress to date?

20. What could you have done to accelerate this progress?

21. Why didn't you do this?

Personal Effectiveness

1. How would you describe yourself?

2. What kind of adjectives would others use to describe you?

3. What are your strengths?

4. In what areas do you need improvement?

5. What are you doing to improve in these areas?

6. How have your past supervisors described you?

7. What have historically been cited as your major strengths?

8. What have historically been cited as areas in which you need to improve? Why?

9. What major changes and improvements have you brought in your last job?

10. Why were these important?

11. How could you have been more effective in your past job?

12. What additional things could you have done to improve your overall impact and performance?

13. Why didn't you do these things?

14. Tell me about your last performance evaluation.

15. What was your last performance rating? Why?

16. If I were to contact each of your past bosses, what would they tell me about your past performance?

17. What plans do you have for improving your effectiveness?

18. In your last job, beyond your normal job responsibilities, what additional major projects did you undertake?

19. How did these extra projects come about?

20. What were the results?

21. In your career to date, what do you consider to be your most significant accomplishment? Why?

22. What was your second most important accomplishment?

23. Why was this important?

24. What is the single most important thing that you could do to improve your overall effectiveness?

Managerial Leadership

1. How would you describe your management style?

2. What are the methods and techniques that you employ when managing others?

3. How effective are these?

4. What results have you gotten?

5. How would your subordinates describe you as a manager?

6. In what areas would they be complimentary?

7. What areas would they likely cite as areas in which you could improve your effectiveness as a manager?

8. What would they say about these areas? Why?

9. How would you describe your management philosophy?

10. What do you see as the major role of management? Why?

11. What is the proper balance between managerial control and employee independence?

12. How do you motivate employees? What kinds of things do you do?

13. What methods do you use to monitor and direct department results?

14. How do you deal with employee performance issues?

15. What methods do you use?

16. Describe your management planning process.

17. How do you go about planning for department results?

18. Who is involved in your planning process?

19. In what ways do you involve them?

20. On a scale of one to ten (ten, high), where would you rate yourself as a manager? Why?

21. How could you improve your overall managerial effectiveness?

This concludes the chapter on interviewing. You should now agree that there is much you can do to dramatically refine your interviewing skills and readiness. With a little patience, good planning, and hard work, it is quite possible to substantially improve your interview effectiveness, and assure a very real competitive advantage in the interview process.

Being an interviewee who can skillfully market his/her overall capability, is one thing; being adept at evaluating the interviewer, is quite another. This is the subject of the next chapter.

12

Negotiating

This chapter deals with the subject of negotiating the job offer. If you are to conclude the job hunting process with an acceptable offer, you must learn the fundamentals of negotiating. Lack of this understanding will cause you to be inept at this critical phase of the job search process, and could cause all of your hard work to be for nothing, should you fail. Failure, in this sense, means either being presented with an unacceptable offer or scaring the employer away with what might be considered unreasonable demands. Both situations, in most cases, can be avoided with a little advance planning and strategy.

This chapter will provide you with some basic strategy that should prove helpful in designing and executing effective job offer negotiations. It will give you a basis for determining a fair offer amount, and for effective presentation of this information to the employer. Likewise, it will explore the offer from the employer's standpoint and provide you with insight concerning the factors that tend to shape the employer's thinking when formulating an employment offer. Having this broad understanding should be helpful in formulating an offer strategy that will contribute to achievement of successful results for both parties.

DETERMINING THE EMPLOYER'S LIMITS

The first step in formulating an effective negotiation strategy is to determine the salary range within which the employer must operate. It is very important, where possible, to establish these limitations in advance of the actual negotiation process.

Most companies will not make an offer at, or near, the top of the salary range for the position. If they do, you should have some concern. Specifically, how is this going to affect your future salary treatment? Chances are, not too well.

If you are dealing with a third party (i.e., employment agency or executive search firm), the job of finding out the salary range of the position will likely be a bit easier. Most, if they know, will share this information with you; but you've got to ask them for it. Some executive search firms, because they have been retained by the employer, may be unwilling to disclose this information on the basis that it may prejudice the negotiating process. For example, if the salary range of the position is $80,000 to $110,000 and you are now earning $70,000, knowing the range maximum may cause you to ask for considerably more than you would have otherwise.

The fact that some of these firms may be unwilling to provide you with salary range information should not stop you from asking. Since this is vital to your negotiating strategy, you shouldn't hesitate to ask. In most cases you will find that these firms, in the interest of putting the deal together, will be willing to share this information with you. If, for some reason, they are unaware of what the salary range is, ask them to find out.

Where there is no third party involved in the process, or where the third party is unwilling to disclose the salary range, you may need to secure this data from the employer directly. In such cases, the employer may be somewhat reluctant to share this information on the basis that you will use it to improve your own negotiating position. Although this strikes to the truth of the matter, the employer can usually be made to feel a little more comfortable with your request, if it is properly positioned. Here is a tactic that you might try:

> Jane, what is the salary range for this position? I would prefer to avoid the situation where I might be hired near or at the range maximum. My experience has been that being compensated at this level frequently leads to future salary administration problems, making it difficult to be appropriately compensated for above average or outstanding performance. Such a situation would concern me.

This type of request seems quite reasonable and will usually elicit a fairly direct response from the employer. On the other hand, some employers have a policy that prohibits disclosure of salary range information to employees. (Fortunately, such companies are in the minority.) If this is the case, however, and the company representative is unwilling to disclose salary facts, here is another strategy that you might employ:

> Look, Jane, I can appreciate that it is against company policy to disclose salary range information, and I don't want to make you uncomfortable with this request. I'm sure, however, that you can appreciate my concerns, as well. Maybe there is a creative solution to this. Perhaps, without disclosing the actual range, you can tell me where my current salary is, relative to the total range. For example, in which quartile does it fall—first, second, third or fourth? Approximately where would it be slotted?

This is a reasonable request, and you have provided good grounds for wanting to know this information. Considering the circumstances, and the way that you have framed your request, it would be very difficult for the company representative to continue to withhold salary information from you without risking the relationship, and potentially jeopardizing the recruiting process. If the employer has any possible interest in your candidacy, it will be most difficult to refuse your request. At this point in the process, you are still somewhat in the driver's seat and have some leverage. Once the actual negotiations start, however, it it too late to request this information, and would be inappropriate to do so.

Now that you have acquired some information concerning the salary range, you are in a more informed position to formulate a successful negotiating strategy. Without this, you have no basis for intelligently pegging a sensible compensation figure, and you are totally at the mercy of the employer.

When formulating your salary request, it is important to realize that employers, for the most part, prefer to make offers that are at, or below, the salary range midpoint. In this way, they can provide the new hire with ample room for salary growth, based upon performance and contribution, and not have to worry about future salary administration problems. The higher in the range they must go to attract a suitable candidate, the greater is the concern for future salary administration issues. This is particularly true when there is no identifiable promotional opportunity to which the candidate can be promoted short range. The higher your current salary is in relationship to the employer's salary range, therefore, the more you may want to shave the amount of increase that you are requesting. If you are too high in the range, and are requesting too much, you could price yourself out of the market, and no offer may be forthcoming.

If, on the other hand, you are at or below the minimum of the employer's salary range, you have considerably more latitude. Percentage wise, in this case, you will want to ask for a substantial salary increase, realizing the employer can afford flexibility. If you are extremely well-qualified, employers will wish to avoid the possibility of some other company sweeping you away with a better offer in the future. There is, therefore, added incentive for the employer to increase the ante. This is especially true if you are in a high demand discipline.

Position in salary range is a factor that has significant influence on what the employer is willing to offer in the way of compensation. Although salary range is, by far, the most significant factor affecting the employer's decision, you need to be aware that there are several other factors as well. Let's take a look at some of these.

OTHER FACTORS AFFECTING COMPENSATION

On the employer's side of the equation, there are a number of factors, other than salary range, that will impact the salary amount offered to a successful candidate. These factors are:

1. Internal salary equity

2. Availability of other qualified candidates

3. Difficulty in filling position

4. Length of time position has been open

5. Criticalness of filling position

6. Level of interest in candidate

7. Candidate's level of interest

8. Availability of future promotional opportunities

9. Candidate's potential for future promotion

Internal salary equity refers to the relationship of the candidate's salary to the members of the existing work group who are at the same level. Employers are concerned with upsetting the apple cart by hiring outsiders at significantly higher compensation levels than members of the current work group, unless such differential is

n the basis of qualifications and experience level. It
difficult, for example, to hire a Ph.D. with four years
?, at $60,000, if the other Ph.D.s in the group average six
ус... эхperience and are making only $50,000. To do so would
cause a serious inequity, and create the potential for dissension
should the other work group members discover this fact. In preparing your negotiating strategy, you should be aware of the back-
grounds and experience levels of your peer group, and should take
time to estimate their probable earnings levels.

Another factor affecting the employer's decision on compensation
is the difficulty in filling the position. If there is a healthy supply of
qualified candidates on the market and the position has only been
open for a short period, you should assume that the employer will
be less receptive to a large increase over your current salary level. If
there are very few qualified persons available and the position has
been open for a long time, the employer may be more flexible on
the salary issue. During the interview, therefore, you should attempt to get a feel for this. Here are some questions to use in
acquiring this information:

1. How long has this position been open?

2. How many candidates have you interviewed?

3. How many candidates are you actively considering?

4. By when would you expect to be making an offer on this
   position?

5. How important is it to fill this position shortly?

Answers to questions such as these can go a long way toward telling
you how well you stack up against the competition, or if there is any
competition at all. Obviously, the less the competition and the
greater the need to fill the position, the more flexible the employer is
likely to be on salary. Conversely, the stiffer the competition and the
less the urgency to fill the position, the less flexible the employer

will be on the subject of compensation. You need to get a good fix on these factors when formulating your offer strategy.

Interest level is also a factor in determining one's negotiating strategy. The stronger the employer's interest in the candidate, the higher the offer amount that the candidate can usually command. Conversely, the lower the interest level of the employer, the lower will be the offer. You must be attentive to the employer's interest level in you.

Another factor that influences the employer's decision on salary offer is the degree of job interest shown by the candidate. If the candidate is clearly excited about the position and communicates this to the employer, the employer will likely shave the offer a bit. On the other hand, where the candidate has expressed interest in the position, but implied that he or she was also considering other things, the employer may be more prone to go in with a higher offer amount in an effort to cement the deal. As part of your negotiation strategy, therefore, you will want to keep your powder dry. Express interest in the position, but don't telegraph your excitement, if you want to get the employer's highest offer. On the other hand, if the competition is stiff and you really want the job, by all means, express your excitement and enthusiasm for the position. In this case, getting a slightly lower offer is well worth assuring yourself a job offer.

Promotability is also a factor affecting compensation level. If the candidate appears to have good potential for promotion beyond the current job, and should a promotional opportunity be readily identifiable, the employer will usually be a little more lenient about compensation. In such cases, the employer will have little concern about making an offer that is high in the salary range. On the other hand, should the candidate have excellent promotional potential, and should there be no identifiable position available for future promotion, the employer will tend to shave the offer, hoping to forestall future salary administration problems. Likewise, if the candidate should appear to have little promotability potential beyond the position for which he or she would be hired, the employer will normally opt for more conservative salary treatment. The employer is concerned about having enough room in the current salary range to keep the new hire satisfied for a fairly long period of time.

As you can see, there are several factors other than just salary range that must be taken into consideration when determining your negotiating strategy. You should carefully think your way through each of these factors before deciding on your target compensation level for negotiation purposes. Judicious consideration of these factors, along with the salary range information that you previously collected, should leave you with a fairly good insight on how the employer is likely to view the structuring of the employment offer. This should help you to zero in on the maximum amount the employer is likely to offer. The other side of the equation is determining the minimum amount that you are willing to accept.

YOUR ROCK-BOTTOM PRICE

Once you have estimated the maximum amount the employer is likely to offer, the next step in preparing your negotiation strategy is to determine the minimum salary that you would be willing to accept. Although in rare cases you might be willing to accept a salary reduction for a given job, usually you are looking for an increase in compensation level. The theory here is that, in addition to increasing the satisfaction derived from *psychic* income, most persons are looking to increase *capital* income, as well.

It should be pointed out that an increase in gross income does not, in itself, assure an increase in net disposable income (i.e., actual buying power). There are, in fact, a number of cost variables that can convert what appears on the surface to be a gain, into an actual loss of substantial proportions. This is particularly so when one is relocating to a new area in order to accept the job. Without some careful analysis, you can be in for a rude awakening.

The key to understanding whether a given offer is financially attractive, requires you to make a comparison between net disposable income in the old job and location with net disposable income in the new job and location. A simple comparison of gross income amounts, unfortunately, won't suffice.

In order to facilitate a comparison, consider the following formula. This formula should be used twice—once to calculate current net disposable income in the current job and location, and second, to calculate net disposable income in the new job and location. Comparing these two net disposable income amounts should provide you with a determination of your actual gains or losses in accepting a given employment offer.

In applying this formula, there are a few subtleties to keep in mind:

1. Both state and local income taxes are deductible from federal income tax. The number used for federal income tax in this formula must be adjusted accordingly.

2. Mortgage interest, real estate tax, personal property tax, state excise tax, and state sales tax may also be deductible from federal income taxes. Check with your tax advisor, and adjust the federal tax calculated in this formula.

3. To reflect an accurate housing comparison, you must adjust your new location housing costs to reflect comparable housing size in your new location. Thus, if you now have a 2,500 square foot house in your current location, the new housing costs must also reflect the cost of a similar 2,500 square foot house in the new location. Contact with two or three realtors in the new location should help you get realistic estimates. (Note: The new employer should not be expected to help you finance the cost of a larger

Net Disposable Income Comparison
Old Location

Gross income (salary, bonus, other) $_____

  Less Income taxes
- Federal $_____
- State   _____
- Local   _____
- Total   _____

  Less Housing costs
- Mortgage Interest   _____
- Real Estate Taxes   _____
- Homeowners Insurance   _____
- Heat   _____
- Water   _____
- Electricity   _____
- Total   _____

  Less Cost of benefits
- Life Insurance   _____
- Medical Insurance   _____
- Disability Insurance   _____
- Dental Insurance   _____
- Retirement Plan   _____
- Other Benefits   _____
- Total   _____

  Less Miscellaneous
- Personal Property Tax   _____
- State Excise Tax   _____
- State Sales Tax Estimate   _____
- Commuting Costs   _____
- Automobile Insurance   _____
- Other   _____
- Total   _____

Less Total expenses $_____

Net disposable income $_____

Net Disposable Income Comparison
New Location

Gross income (salary, bonus, other) $_____

  Less Income taxes

        Federal $_____

        State   _____

        Local   _____

        Total   _____

  Less Housing costs

        Mortgage Interest   _____

        Real Estate Taxes   _____

        Homeowners Insurance   _____

        Heat   _____

        Water   _____

        Electricity   _____

        Total   _____

  Less Cost of benefits

        Life Insurance   _____

        Medical Insurance   _____

        Disability Insurance   _____

        Dental Insurance   _____

        Retirement Plan   _____

        Other Benefits   _____

        Total   _____

  Less Miscellaneous

        Personal Property Tax   _____

        State Excise Tax   _____

        State Sales Tax Estimate   _____

        Commuting Costs   _____

        Automobile Insurance   _____

        Other   _____

        Total   _____

Less Total expenses $_____

Net disposable income $_____

house. All calculations should therefore be based upon the same size and style house in both locations.)

By experimenting with different gross income figures and using the formula supplied here, it should be possible for you to determine the amount of gross salary increase that will be required for you to break even or show some improvement in net disposable income. Because of the potential for significant variation in cost of living factors between different locations, however, it is very important for you to go through this analysis in advance of negotiating your offer. If you find these costs are significantly higher in the new location, you have some fairly powerful ammunition to support your increased salary demands during the negotiation process. On the other hand, if the cost of living in the new location is significantly less than the old location, you may find that little or no increase in gross income will be necessary for you to improve your net disposable income and increase your purchasing power.

This calculation should provide you with useful insight regarding the amount of the offer that you will require as rock-bottom to make this particular move financially palatable.

ACTUAL NEGOTIATIONS

You should now have a good idea of the maximum amount that the employer will be willing to offer. You also know your own rock-bottom price, as well.

At the beginning of actual negotiations, you will likely be asked to indicate the level of offer that you are looking for. In all cases you should respond with an amount that you believe to be slightly in excess of the maximum amount that you believe they are prepared to offer. In this way, you have allowed sufficient room for negotiations.

When responding to this request, it is usually a good idea to provide some underlying rationale for the amount that you are requesting. This way, you don't appear as though you are being arbitrary. Such rationale could be as follows:

> Sam, although it may, at first, seem a little high, I feel that I'm going to need an offer of about $80,000 to make this interesting. Some research that I have done on cost of living differential between here and Chicago suggests that I will need another $6,000 in gross income just to break even. Since this position represents an increase in accountability over my past job, I would also like to see some increase in overall income, in the neighborhood of $5,000. I am thus requesting a total increase of $11,000, taking my salary from $69,000 to $80,000. Backing out cost of living differential, this represents an increase of only $5,000 or 7.2 percent, which to me seems reasonable. What do you think?

Notice how effectively the cost of living data was used. In addition, because of the detailed prepared analysis, you are ready to substantiate your claims regarding living costs. You are pointing out that your real gain is only 7.2 percent versus the 15.9 percent suggested by the overall $11,000 increase. The distinction, of course, is the difference in cost of living between your current community and that of Chicago. This makes the request appear considerably more compatible than had you offered no rationale for the compensation request.

Should the employer indicate that this is more than they are prepared to offer, you may want to qualify them further by determining how much they are willing to pay and why. Here is how that might be handled:

Employer: That's a lot more than we were thinking of.

Candidate: Well, what did you have in mind?

Employer: We were thinking of an offer in the $75,000 to $77,000 range.

Candidate: I see. Quite frankly, that's a little less than I was hoping for. Can you share with me some of your thinking behind this amount?

Employer: Well, we are concerned about creating some internal salary inequities. You see, two of our other employees, who have comparable credentials to your own, are earning $75,000. As a result, we would feel most uncomfortable going beyond the $75,000 to $77,000 range.

Candidate: Although this is a little lower than I had hoped, I can appreciate the position this puts you in. Why don't we agree to $75,000 then?

In this case it should be evident that the employer is not prepared to go higher with its offer. The major issue here is salary inequity, and although the company may be able to tolerate a $2,000 differential, it highly unlikely that they will risk the potential for internal unrest by going much higher. If you attempt to push the offer much higher, it is possible that you could jeopardize the whole deal.

As you can see, when the employer counters with a lower offer, you should always ask why. If there is no good underlying reason for low-balling the offer, you can usually fairly safely assume that this lower offer is just a part of their negotiating strategy, and they are simply trying to get you down from your original request. In such cases, there is usually some room on the up side for you to negotiate further. Perhaps, you might suggest splitting the difference.

On the other hand, when the employer is willing to share the rationale behind a lower offer, you will want to listen carefully. Listen not only to the reason behind the lower offer, but to tone as well. If there is a good reason stated for the lower offer and the tone of the conversation suggests that the employer is fairly determined about this, then there is little likelihood that there is room for further negotiations. You can usually assume that you are already at their maximum number and the probability is high that you will kill negotiations if you try to push things much further.

In summary then, the basic rules to remember when negotiating an offer are:

1. Determine position salary range.

2. Be alert to other factors that could affect the amount the employer is willing to offer.

3. Based on the first two items, try to estimate the maximum amount the employer is likely to offer.

4. Determine through careful analysis, including cost of living factors, the minimum amount you are prepared to accept.

5. Always request slightly more than you believe the employer is prepared to offer.

6. Always provide the employer with some underlying rationale for your offer request.

7. When the employer counters with an offer that is below the level of your request, ask for the rationale. (Listen for both validity of this rationale as well as the employer's tone.)

8. When rationale for this lower offer seems somewhat weak, and the employer's tone doesn't suggest strong resolve, assume there is further room for negotiations. Either stick with your original request (if not much higher than the counter offer) or suggest an acceptable compromise figure (if there is a significant differential between your request and the counter offer).

9. When the rationale provided by the employer seems fairly solid and the tone suggests a strong resolve to go no higher than the counter offer amount, it is probably unwise to attempt to negotiate further if you are truly interested in the position. You will probably want to suggest a compromise amount (probably half way between the two) just to test this resolve, but be prepared to back off quickly should the employer indicate that they have no further flexibility. At this point, you are probably at the *take it or leave it* stage.

MOVING COSTS

When negotiating with the employer, an area that may be overlooked by the inexperienced job hunter is moving expense reimbursement. If acceptance of the position will require you to relocate, this is not a consideration that you should ignore. The costs of moving can be enormous, and can prove financially devastating if not at least in part paid for by the employer. A real estate commission of 7 percent on a $200,000 home, for example, can cost you $14,000 alone. Shipment of your household goods could easily be another $6,000 to $10,000, dependent upon the size of your house and the distance of the move. Already your costs could be $20,000 to $24,000, without so much as blinking an eye.

So that you are not caught by surprise, here is a list of moving expense items for which you should be prepared to negotiate with the employer:

Moving Expense

1. Househunting trip to the new location.

2. Shipment of household goods (and storage, if necessary).

3. Temporary living expenses (while waiting to move into new quarters).

4. Double housing expense (if needing to carry mortgages and other expenses on both the old and the new location houses at the same time).

5. Third party home buying assistance (if you anticipate difficulty in selling your old location residence).

6. Reimbursement of sale closing costs (on sale of your old location house).

7. Reimbursement of purchase closing costs (on purchase of new location house).

8. Reimbursement of lease penalty fee or forfeited rent (should you be renting and need to break your lease agreement).

9. Tax gross-up for all taxable moving expenses, reimbursed to you by the employer. (Note: Certain moving expense reimbursements constitute taxable income under federal tax laws.)

It doesn't require a very high IQ to realize that these moving expenses can be substantial. It is important, therefore, that you take time to estimate them in advance of your negotiations, so that you have some idea as to what you are dealing with in terms of total price tag. Such analysis will also serve to allow you to be more definitive when entering into discussions with the employer on this matter.

It is difficult to suggest a specific negotiating strategy for moving expense reimbursement, since there is considerable variance in what companies are willing to pay. Even within the same company, there may be considerable variance in reimbursement, dependent upon job level. It is strongly recommended, therefore, that you investigate this area thoroughly during the interview process so that you have some advance knowledge of the company's position. Here are some questions you might use:

1. What is your policy regarding moving expense reimbursement for this level position?

2. Specifically, what expenses is the company willing to reimburse?

3. What items of expense are considered to be negotiable?

4. What items are generally considered nonnegotiable? Why?

Answers to these and similar questions will go a long way toward formulating a reasonable negotiating strategy for moving expense reimbursement. Without these answers, you'll be groping in the dark.

GET IT IN WRITING

Whatever the final package you end up negotiating with the employer, there is one critical thing to remember: Get it in writing! There are numerous details covered verbally during the negotiating process, and sometimes people have short memories regarding the specifics of the final agreement. To avoid disagreement and potential unpleasantness, it is in your best interest to request that the employer confirm the details of the offer in writing. In this way, there can be little confusion as to what was said and agreed upon. This is a very reasonable request, and one that the majority of employers will willingly grant.

13

Selecting the Right Employer

When evaluating and selecting the company for whom you would like to work, there are essentially four areas that require careful consideration and evaluation. They are:

1. Stability and growth of organization

2. Your technical fit

3. Organizational compatibility

4. Opportunities for growth and advancement

Each of these is a critical factor that will substantially impact your future probability for success and happiness in the job and, therefore, deserves careful examination. This chapter is intended to provide you with some methods to examine each of these areas, and enable you to collect the kind of information that is essential to making a solid employment decision.

This is an aspect of the employment process that merits your maximum time and effort. Accepting the wrong offer or going to work for the wrong company can have serious far-reaching implications for your career. Let's, therefore, systematically consider each of these components of the employer evaluation and selection process.

GROWTH AND STABILITY OF FIRM

A little research can go a long way in determining the stability and growth of a prospective employer. Two of the best documents for examining the recent performance history of the organization, are the firm's annual report and the 10-K. Careful review of these two resources will provide some excellent data for observing historical trends. In addition, the annual report will provide information concerning new products, markets, and business strategies that the firm is intending to pursue.

When reviewing the annual report, in particular, you will want to review the ten-year summary of sales and earnings. What has been the trend? Have sales and earnings been on the rise or on the decline? What does the annual report say about the prospects for future growth? If there has been a long term negative trend or a recent dramatic decline, some red flags should go up. What has caused this negative trend? What are the chances it will continue in the future? What are the consequences of such a continuation?

Surely you don't want to accept a job in a company where the future trend appears to be contraction and layoffs. Even if you survive the layoffs, the prospects for future advancement is likely to be rather bleak. Should you accept employment with such a firm, however, you should do so knowing full well that you will likely need to make an additional move at some future point if you are to realize reasonable growth and career advancement.

Other good sources of information concerning the
stability of a firm are trade publications and business
You should plan to spend some time in the periodical
good library to search for recent articles on the firm and its competition.

In addition, the employment interview is a good opportunity to
address many of these areas. Here are some questions that you may
want to ask the employer during the employment interview in order to get a better assessment of the growth and stability factor:

1. What are the prospects for future growth and expansion of
   this company?

2. What is the company's general strategy for future growth
   and expansion?

3. What kinds of new products is the company planning to
   introduce to support this growth strategy?

4. What new markets is the company considering?

5. What plans does the company have for future ventures or
   acquisitions?

6. What expansions are planned for existing products, markets,
   and facilities?

7. What are the major issues that stand in the way of company
   growth and progress?

8. How are these issues being addressed? What is being done
   to resolve them?

9. What kind of annual growth rate do you foresee for the next
   five to ten years? Why?

10. What layoffs or cutbacks has the company experienced dur-
    ing the last five years? Why?

11. Was this work group affected? How? To what degree?

12. Are any employee cutbacks planned or anticipated in the foreseeable future?

13. What effect, if any, would you expect this to have on the position for which I am interviewing?

Having done some thorough advance research on the company, followed by some careful questions during the interview, you should be in a fairly good position to effectively evaluate the prospects for future organizational growth and stability. Although no one has a crystal ball to see into the future, if you have followed this advice, you can be assured that you have done all that you can to determine the future prospects for these important employer evaluation and selection factors.

TECHNICAL FIT

How well are you equipped to handle the technical aspects of the job? From the technical standpoint, is this a good fit for you? Are you going to find the technical work both challenging and professionally satisfying? These are important questions to answer when making an employment decision. Inability to handle the technical work, or dissatisfaction with the technical content of the job, has some very real short-term implications from the career standpoint. Simply put, you'll find yourself on the outside looking in.

The employment interview is perhaps the best place to pick up the kind of information that you will need to make a good decision about the possibility of a good technical fit. Here are some of the key questions that you will need to answer when evaluating this important factor:

1. What are the key ongoing functional accountabilities of this position?

2. What are the major changes that the organization wishes to bring about?

3. What are the key technical problems that need to be solved in order to meet these accountabilities and bring about the desired changes?

4. What specific knowledge and technical skills are needed to solve these key problems?

5. Are my knowledge and technical skills sufficiently strong to allow me to successfully solve these key problems and achieve the results that will be expected of me?

6. How challenged and satisfied will I be in a job that requires me to work on these kinds of problems and use this kind of knowledge and skill?

By asking sufficient questions about job content, job accountabilities, key problems to be addressed, etc., during the employment interview, you should be in an excellent position to gauge your technical fit for the position you are considering.

ORGANIZATIONAL COMPATIBILITY

Technical fit is one thing, but organizational compatibility is yet another. From the technical standpoint you may be exceptionally well-qualified to perform the job, but what if you don't enjoy associating with those with whom you will be working? What if you simply don't fit in?

It is estimated by knowledgeable sources that 85 percent or better of all job failures are not the result of technical inability, but are instead the direct or indirect result of organizational incompatibility. When a person does not align well with the organization or the immediate work group, sooner or later there will be issues. In such cases the individual usually finds himself or herself on the periphery of the group. His or her focus and priorities are different from those of the group. He or she frequently argues with the views of other group members, and is thus described as stubborn, inflexible, argumentive, uncooperative, rebellious, etc. Ideas and plans do not receive the endorsement and support of other group members, and often the necessary resources and support needed for successful performance are not forthcoming from the organization. In the eyes of the organization, the employee is thereby a failure. Interestingly, this has little to do with technical competence. It is a phenomenon of social incompatibility.

It should be evident from this discussion that you will need to evaluate your own compatibility with that of the organization if you want to be sure that you will fit in, and that you will align well with the work group. Here are some questions that will help you evaluate this factor and make a good employment decision:

1. What is the overall business philosophy of the organization?

2. How well does this align with your own business philosophy?

3. What is the predominant philosophy of the immediate work group?

4. What do they consider important? What do they consider unimportant?

5. How well do these align with your personal philosophy and order of priorities?

6. What is the predominant operating style of the immediate work group?

7. What is characteristic about the way this group operates?

8. How well does your personal operating style align with that of this group? What is similar? What is different?

9. Who are the obvious leaders of the work group?

10. In what ways are they similar? How are they different?

11. In what ways are you similar? In what ways are you different?

12. Overall, how well do you align with this group?

13. In what ways will you feel comfortable? In what ways will you feels uncomfortable?

14. What is the probability that you will be organizationally compatible with this group?

As you can see there is much that you can do to forecast the probability of a successful social fit with the organization. The interview should be used to make some careful observations and to ask some key questions to collect information in this area. If you are going to make a good selection, you simply can't afford to leave this to chance.

OPPORTUNITIES FOR GROWTH AND ADVANCEMENT

If you are a person for whom future growth and advancement are important to satisfy your long-range career objectives, you will want to make sure that the new organization will provide for realistic opportunities in this area. In order to effectively evaluate this important factor, you will need to ask some very pointed questions and make some astute observations during the course of the employment interview. Here are some questions that you might use to test the waters:

1. What has been the history of promotions in this department during the last five years?

2. How many promotions have there been?

3. To what kind of positions have these persons been promoted?

4. Where are some of these people today?

5. Assuming good performance, how long might I expect to be in this position?

6. To what positions would I likely progress? Why?

7. What other options might be available? Why?

8. What are the criteria for promotion? How do you determine when a person is ready?

9. What training and development are available to better prepare persons for advancement to the next level?

10. Who was in this position for the shortest period of time? Why?

11. Who was in this position for the longest period of time? Why?

12. What factors affect the length of time that I might be required to spend in this position?

13. What else can you tell me about opportunities for promotion and advancement?

Answers to these questions should provide you with some useful information for accessing promotional opportunities within the companies that you are seriously considering. These questions, or ones similar to them, should clearly be part of your interview repertoire. Without answers to these questions, it will be impossible to evaluate this important employer evaluation and selection factor.

You should now be in an excellent position to evaluate and select the kind of employer, position, and environment that will most fully satisfy your employment needs.

Index